# VULNERABILITY
## IS MY SUPERPOWER

Andrews McMeel Publishing
a division of Andrews McMeel Universal
1130 Walnut Street, Kansas City, Missouri 64106

21 22 23 24 25 TEN 10 9 8 7 6 5 4 3 2 1

ISBN: 978-1-5248-6508-5

Library of Congress Control Number: 2020946072

Editor: Lucas Wetzel
Art Director: Julie Barnes
Production Editor: Jasmine Lim
Production Manager: Tamara Haus

www.andrewsmcmeel.com

# VULNERABILITY IS MY SUPERPOWER

Jackie E. Davis

Andrews McMeel
PUBLISHING®

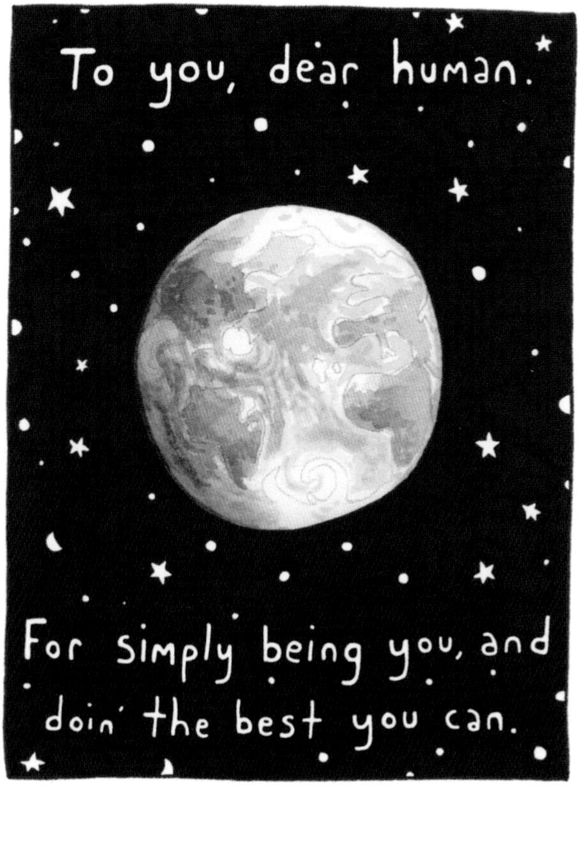
To you, dear human.
For simply being you, and
doin' the best you can.

# Introduction

Vulnerability is my superpower. But it wasn't always.

If you'd asked me even three years ago, I probably would've said silliness was my superpower, and then made a "boing boing" sound as I hopped away. Moments later though, I would've boinged back anxiously and asked, "Did I say something wrong? Are you mad at me? Do you like me?" Because really, self-doubt was my superpower. Or maybe it was my super-deficit.

Either way, it all brought me here.

How did I go from super doubtful to super vulnerable? Gradually, painfully, sloppily, imperfectly. And often with a pencil in my hand and a therapist on speed dial. There were a lot of factors on this journey, and the process is ongoing, but something about making a diary comic was the key.

When I started Underpants and Overbites, I set out to be silly. Basically, the day I was born, I set out to be silly. Silly felt safe. Silly meant I could be my authentic, weird self, but if someone made fun of me, I could pretend I was only joking. No one could take away what I never claimed for myself. Now if I was sincere—about liking something, or wanting something, or believing in something—and then someone called it stupid, that precious thing would crumble before my eyes. I didn't know how to defend what I loved, and I certainly didn't know how to defend myself. So I stayed silly.

I drew silly cows and silly puns and silly characters. One day, a friend suggested I make myself the main character in my comics. I wanted to draw silly stuff, and I did have a pretty silly life, so I decided to give it a shot. After all, silly was safe.

But something happened when I started drawing myself. It was a very gradual process as we got to know each other, but eventually, that little comic character stopped being so silly and started standing up for me. She learned to defend me before I did. She helped me believe in myself. She reframed narratives from belittling ones to empowering ones and showed me the beauty and strength in sincerity. That little character is what makes me feel safe enough to be vulnerable.

So I take it back, vulnerability isn't my superpower; it's hers.

I hope that by reading this book, it can also become yours.

Jackie

# Vulnerability

Vulnerability is my superpower!
I'm so strong, I don't need to pretend I'm strong!
The more I share about myself...
I'm vulnerable!
... the more it can connect other people.
Hey, Sometimes I feel vulnerable too.
Whoa, same.

Now that's pretty super!
Um, your "V" fell off.
and I can see your underwear.
uhh

# Quittin' Time

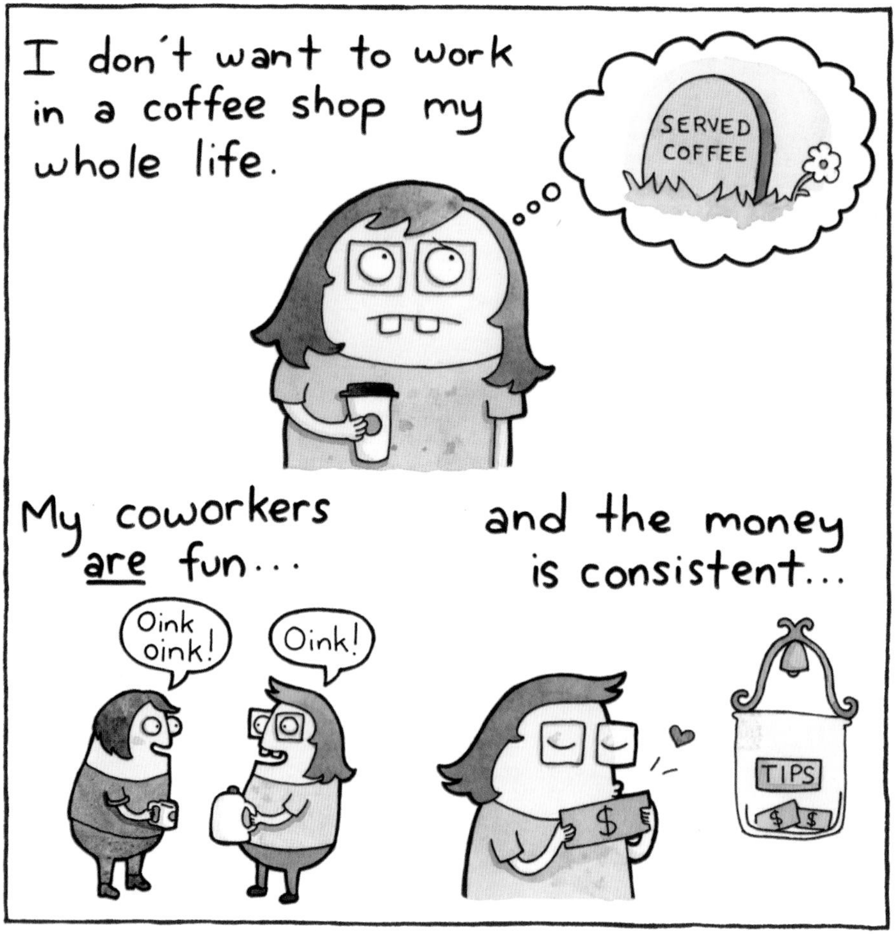

I don't want to work in a coffee shop my whole life.
SERVED COFFEE
My coworkers are fun...
Oink oink!
Oink!
and the money is consistent...
$
TIPS
$ $

But I've worked in coffee shops for 8 years, from the moment I stepped out of art school.

I decided to make coffee for money and art for fun. Eventually people would pay me to make art, right?

Despite how unqualified I was, my confidence was unwavering at the time.*

Glad I didn't sell out and work for a big company.

* no concept of anatomy, perspective, or business

I didn't "sell out", but I didn't make much art. I made coffee.

I often compared myself to practicing artists when I could have been drawing.

I could do that.

100,000 followers?!

Of course they're more successful, they're older.

Sometimes I __would__ use my skills at work, but that never went far.

PUMPKIN LATTE

It took me years to realize someone wasn't going to magically pay me to do what I love.
Are you the barista that likes to doodle?
Why yes!

Eventually I developed more direction.

COMICS

The more I explore through drawing, the more exciting it becomes.

I want to make a living with it...

When I moved to
Rochester 3 years ago,
I set out to draw
my way to a career.

I still had to pay rent, so I served
coffee by day and drew by night.

At times it was exhausting.

SCRIBBLE
SCRIBBLE

But it's hard because I have to go to this pesky place called work.
*sigh* For here or to go?

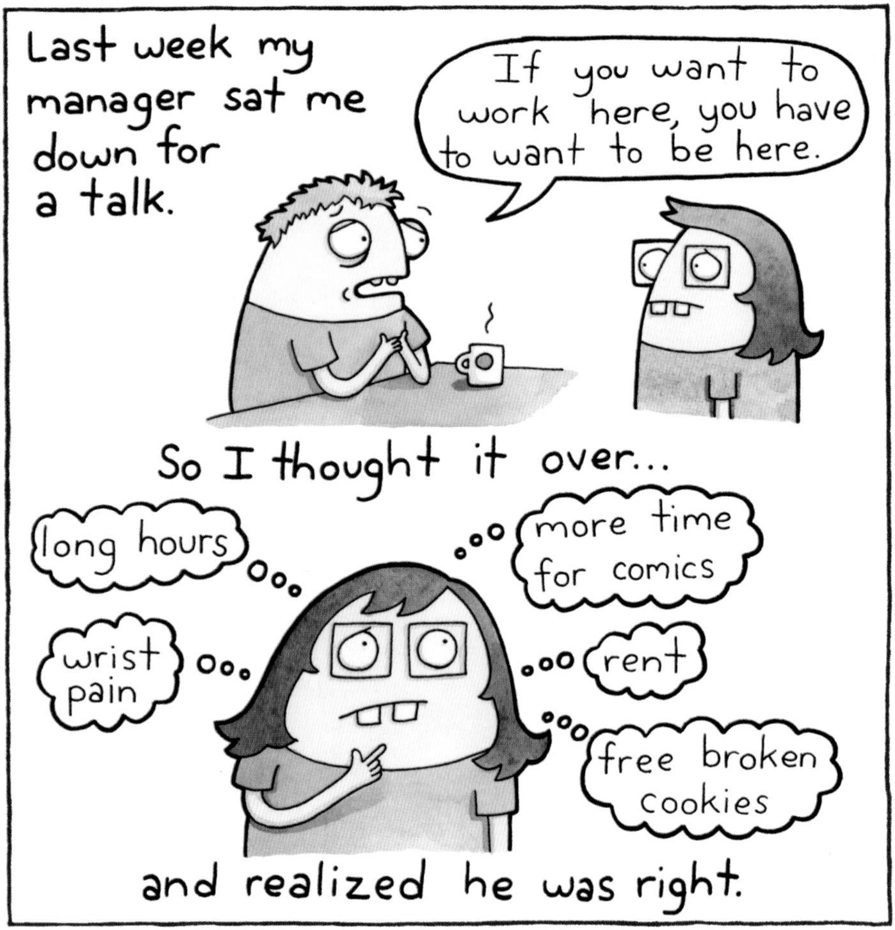
Last week my manager sat me down for a talk.
If you want to work here, you have to want to be here.
So I thought it over...
long hours
more time for comics
wrist pain
rent
free broken cookies
and realized he was right.

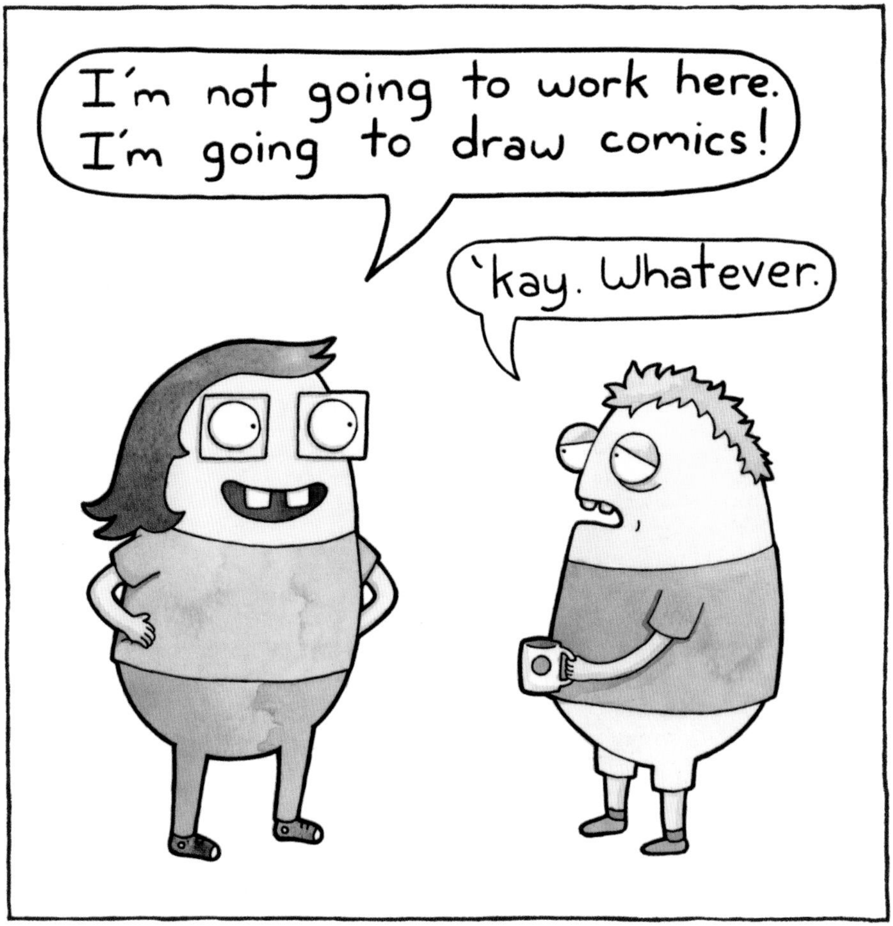
I'm not going to work here. I'm going to draw comics!
`kay. Whatever.

9 Things I LOVE
That NOBODY
Else Does
The mouse living somewhere in my kitchen
Ohh, sounds like you're havin' dinner too.
*rustle rustle*
When a bug flies into my mouth
PTOO
Oops, excuse me!
Gum on the underside of a chair
mmm, so bumpy
Hearing the neighbor blow her nose
*honk honk*

The back middle seat

Dogs wearing cones

Going to the dentist

Floss me extra hard, please.

Turbulence

Weeee

When a toilet seat has been warmed by another butt

## Not Right for Me

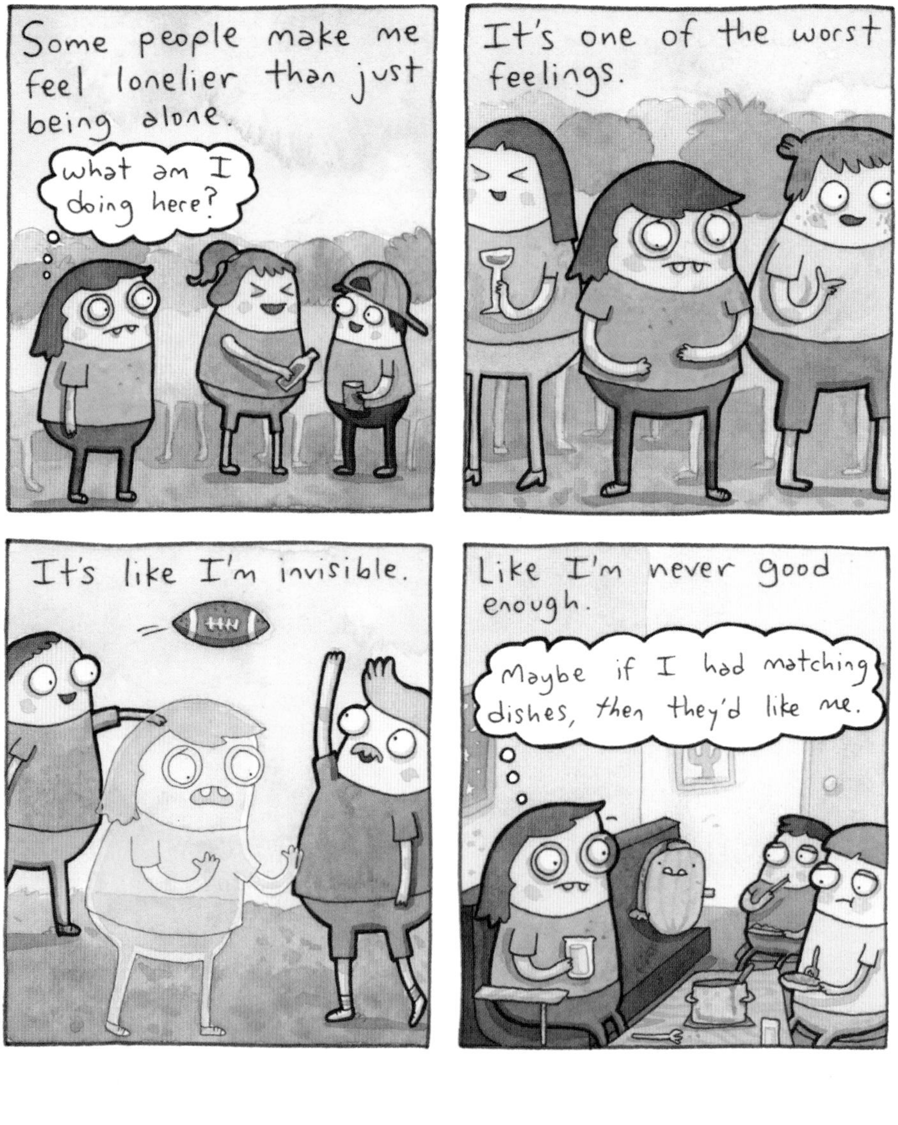
Some people make me feel lonelier than just being alone.
what am I doing here?
It's one of the worst feelings.
It's like I'm invisible.
Like I'm never good enough.
Maybe if I had matching dishes, then they'd like me.

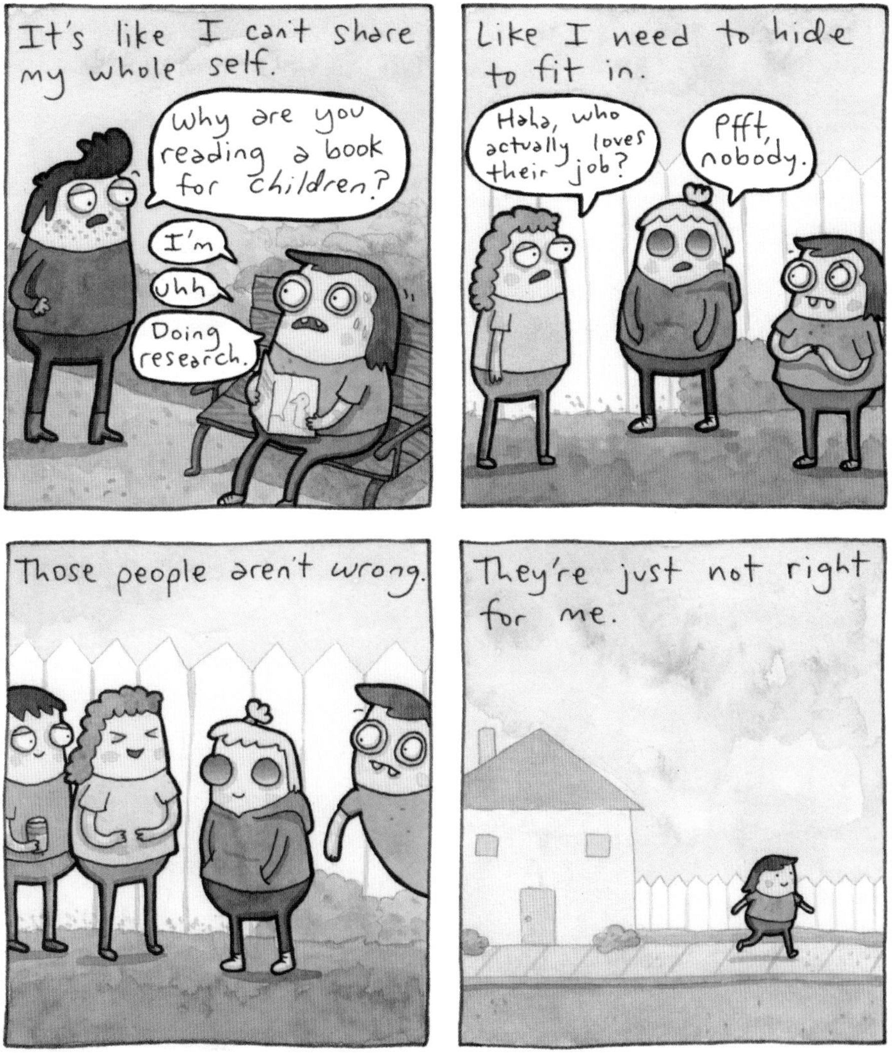
It's like I can't share my whole self.
Why are you reading a book for children?
I'm
uhh
Doing research.
Like I need to hide to fit in.
Haha, who actually loves their job?
Pfft, nobody.
Those people aren't wrong.
They're just not right for me.

# Other Other Days

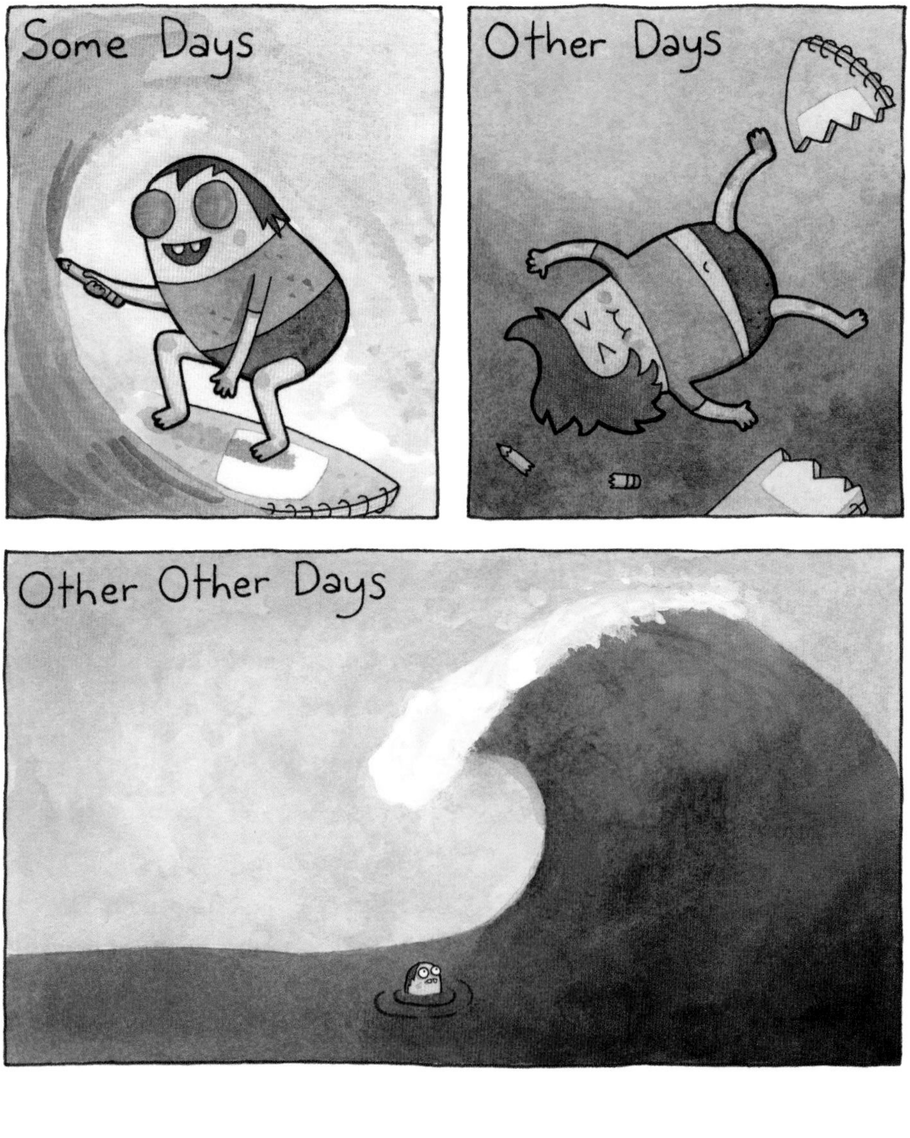
Some Days
Other Days
Other Other Days

*gulp
Getting Started
Hey, it wasn't even locked.

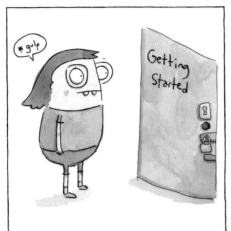

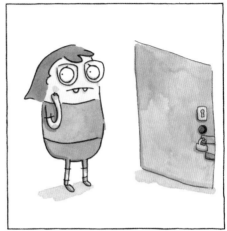

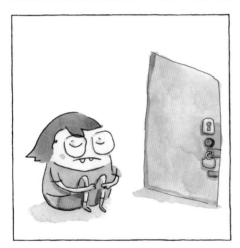

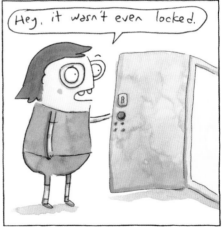

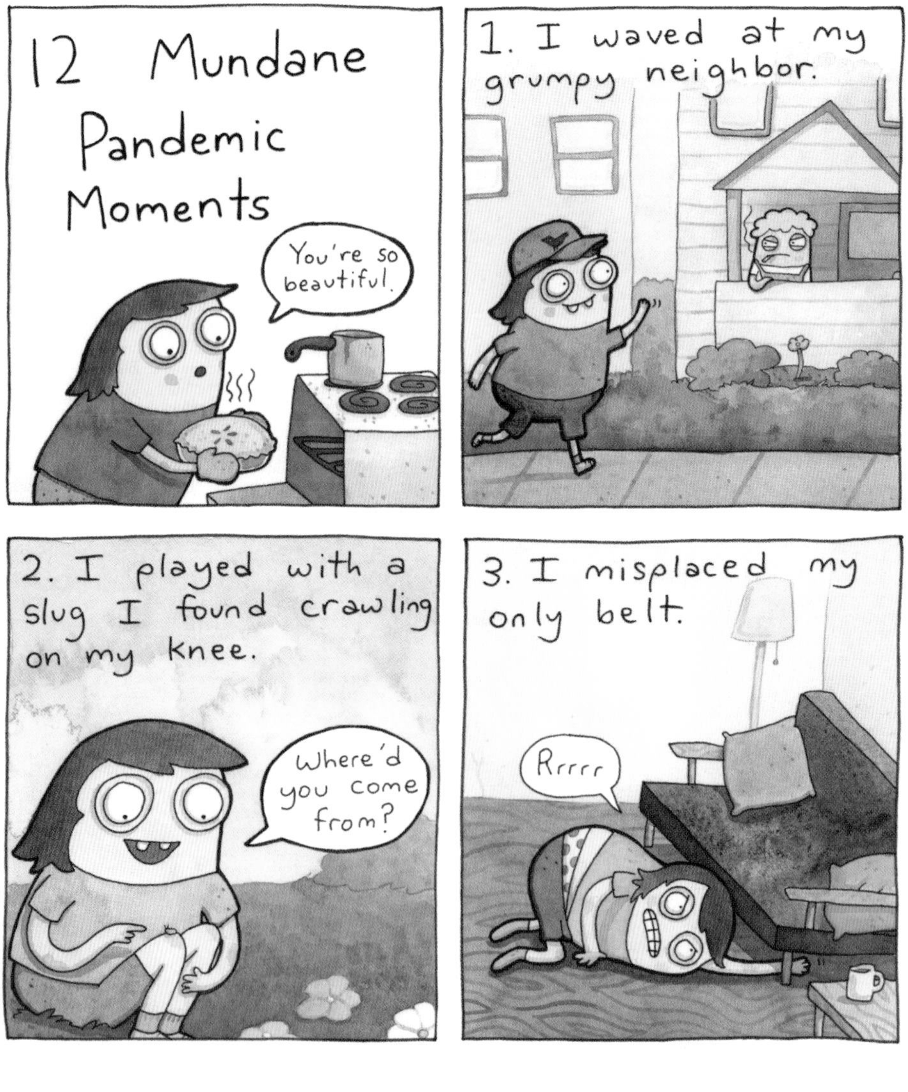
12 Mundane Pandemic Moments
You're so beautiful.
1. I waved at my grumpy neighbor.
2. I played with a slug I found crawling on my knee.
Where'd you come from?
3. I misplaced my only belt.
Rrrrr

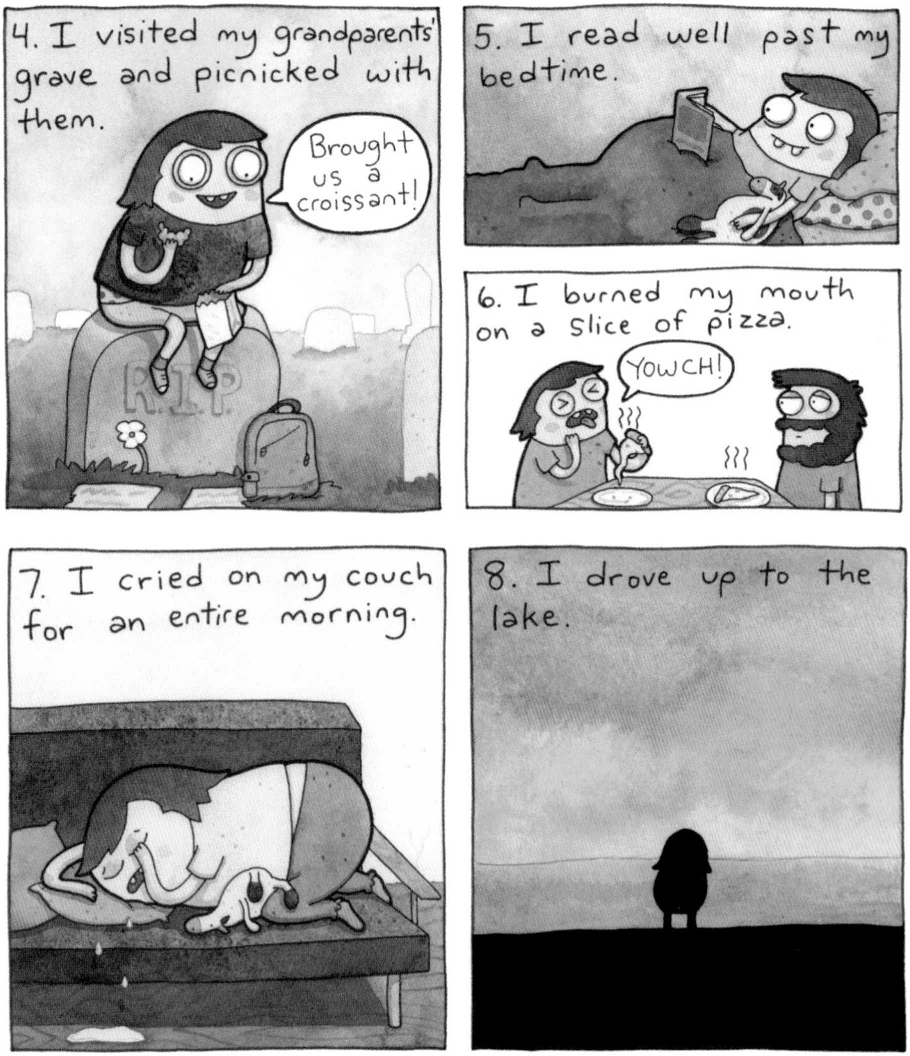
4. I visited my grandparents' grave and picnicked with them.
Brought us a croissant!
R.I.P.
5. I read well past my bedtime.
6. I burned my mouth on a slice of pizza.
YOWCH!
7. I cried on my couch for an entire morning.
8. I drove up to the lake.

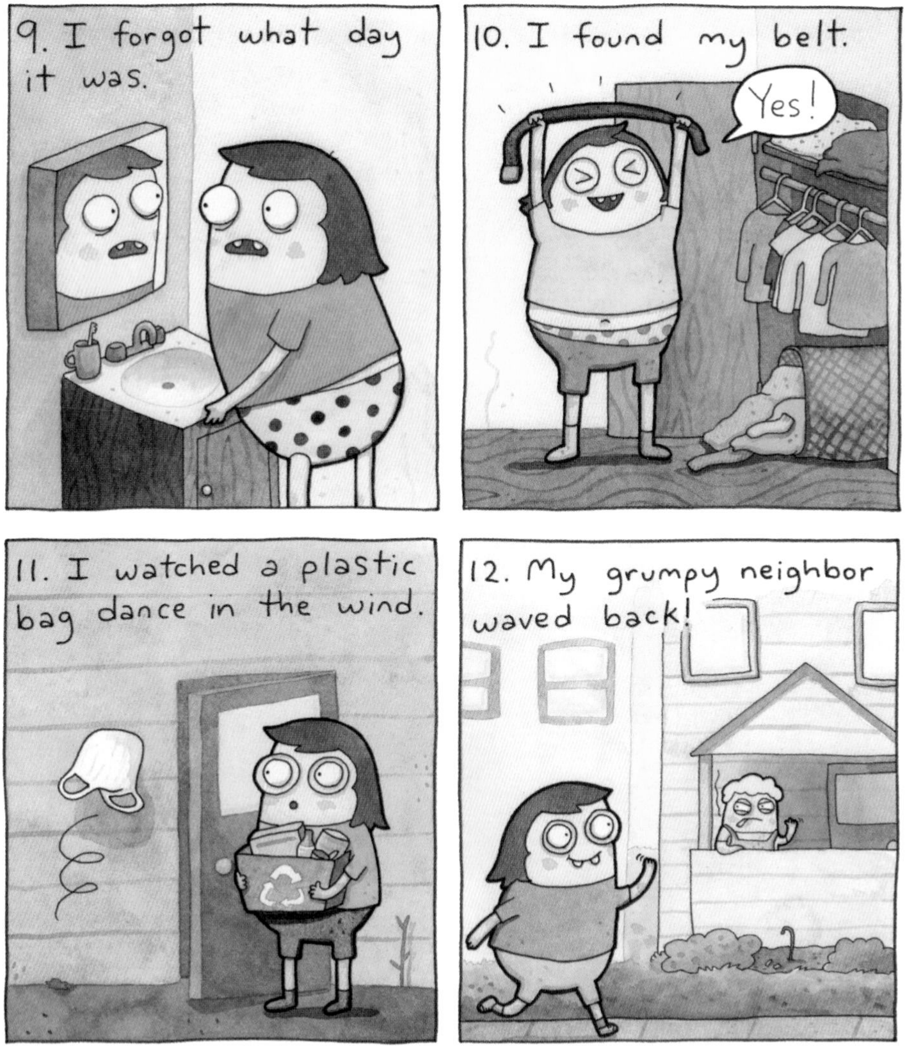
9. I forgot what day it was.
10. I found my belt.
Yes!
11. I watched a plastic bag dance in the wind.
12. My grumpy neighbor waved back!

# Just the Way You Are

Two of my favorite things to hear in the whole world are:

I'm so glad you're here, and
I love you just the way you are.
On good days, I can say them to myself.
On bad days, I can't.

There's always tomorrow.

## Message in a Bottle

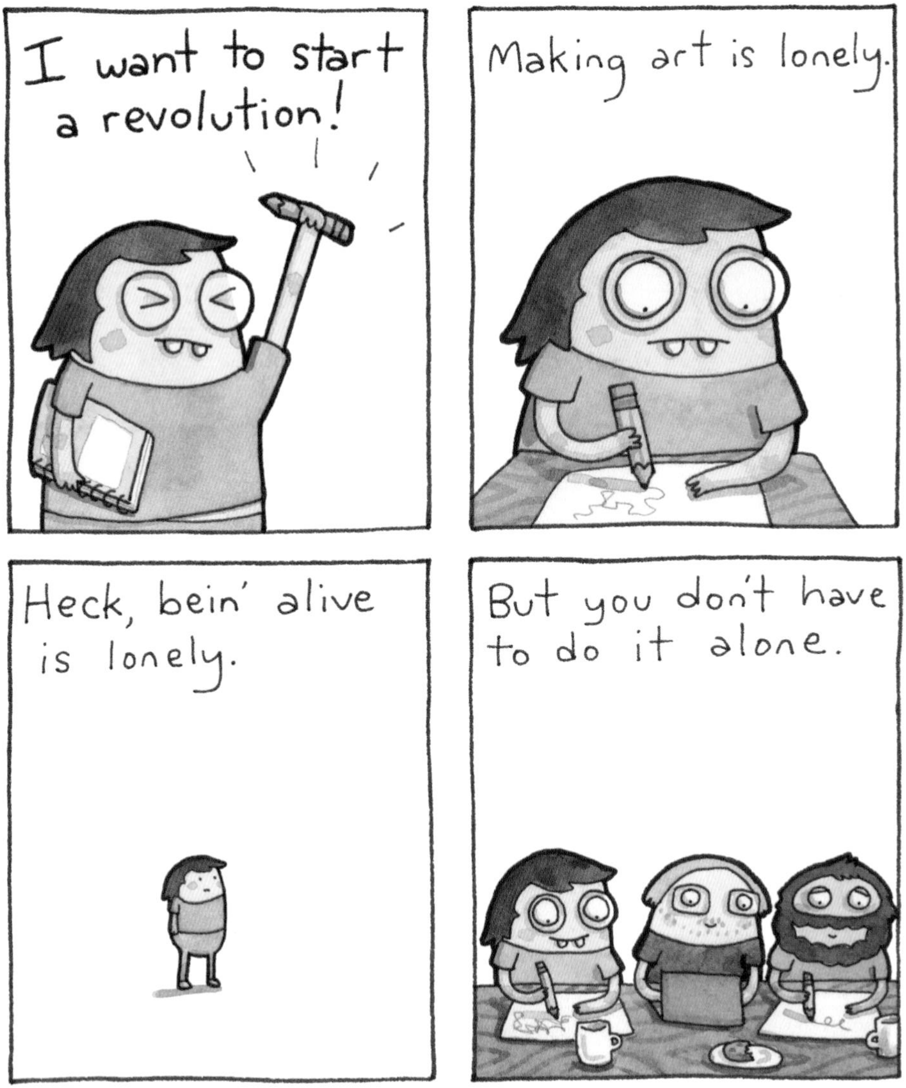
I want to start a revolution!
Making art is lonely.
Heck, bein' alive is lonely.
But you don't have to do it alone.

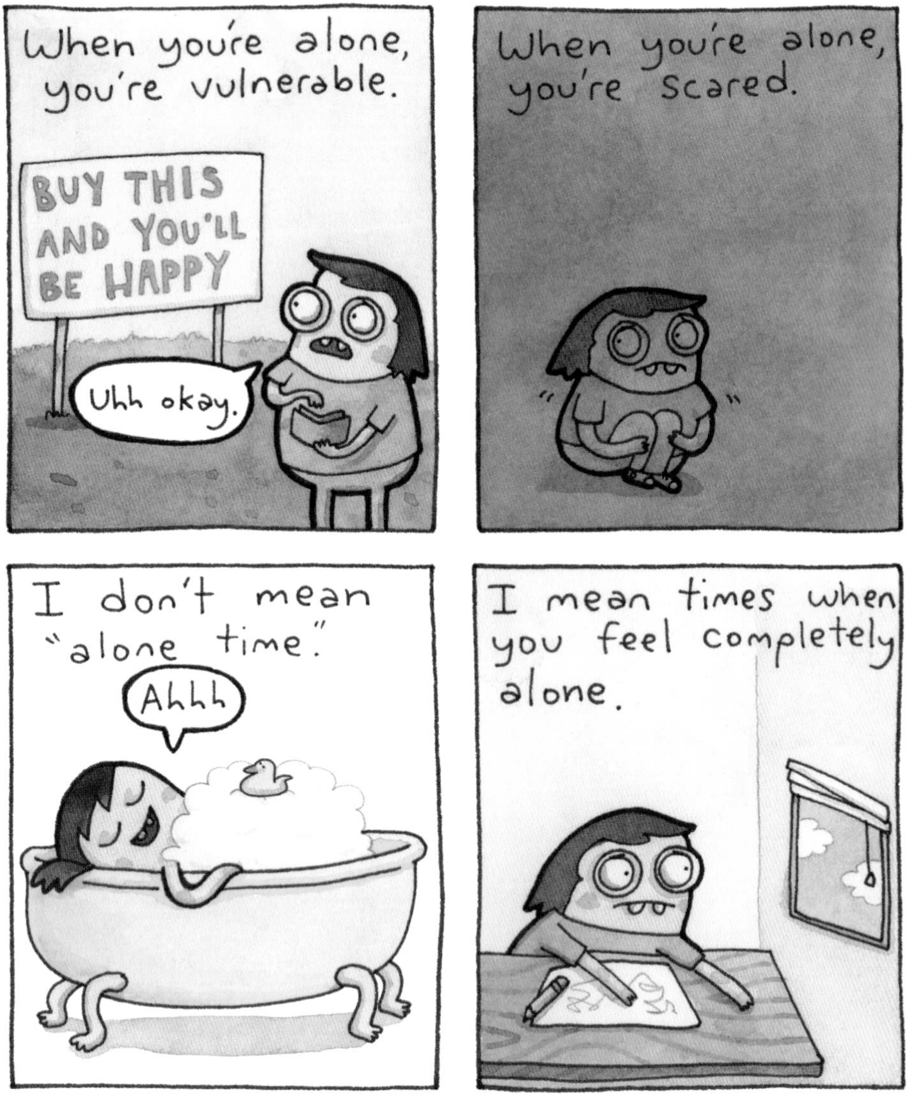
When you're alone, you're vulnerable.
BUY THIS AND YOU'LL BE HAPPY
Uhh okay.
When you're alone, you're scared.
I don't mean "alone time."
Ahhh
I mean times when you feel completely alone.

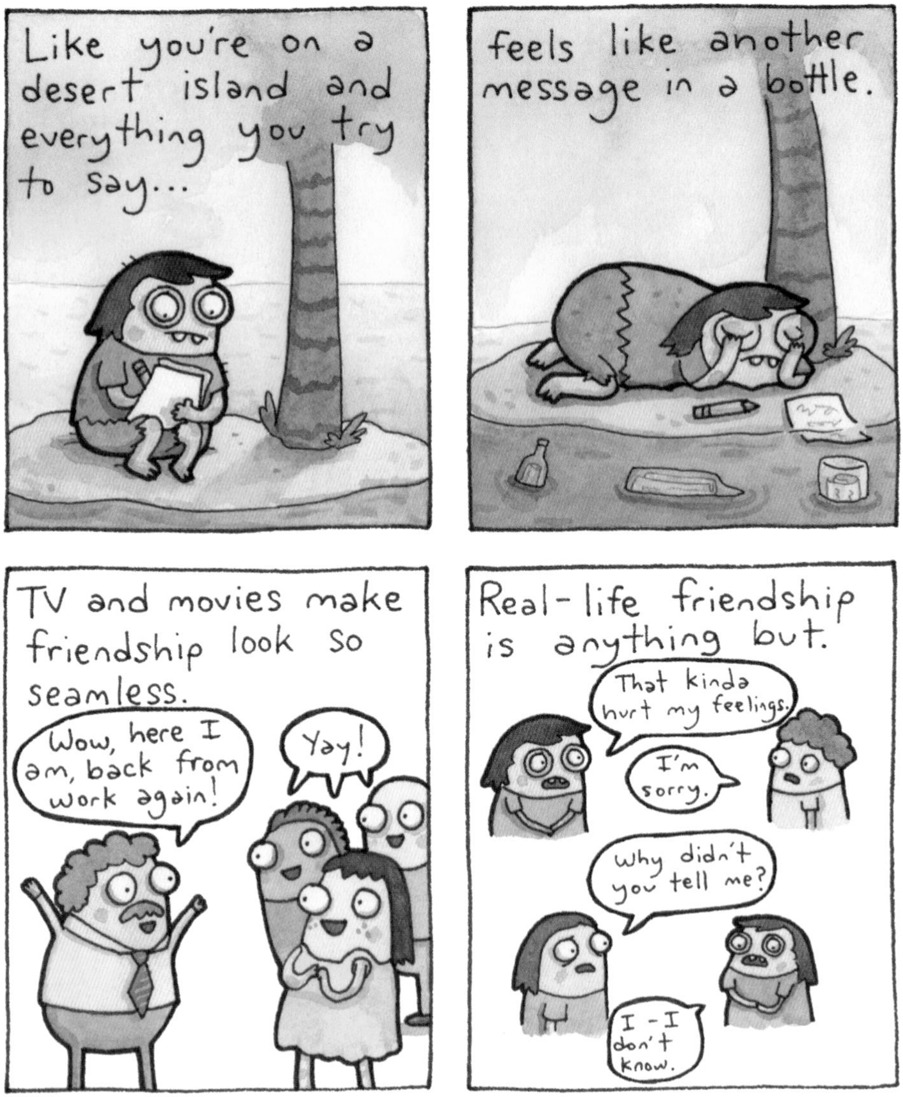
Like you're on a desert island and everything you try to say...
feels like another message in a bottle.
TV and movies make friendship look so seamless.
Wow, here I am, back from work again!
Yay!
Real-life friendship is anything but.
That kinda hurt my feelings.
I'm sorry.
Why didn't you tell me?
I-I don't know.

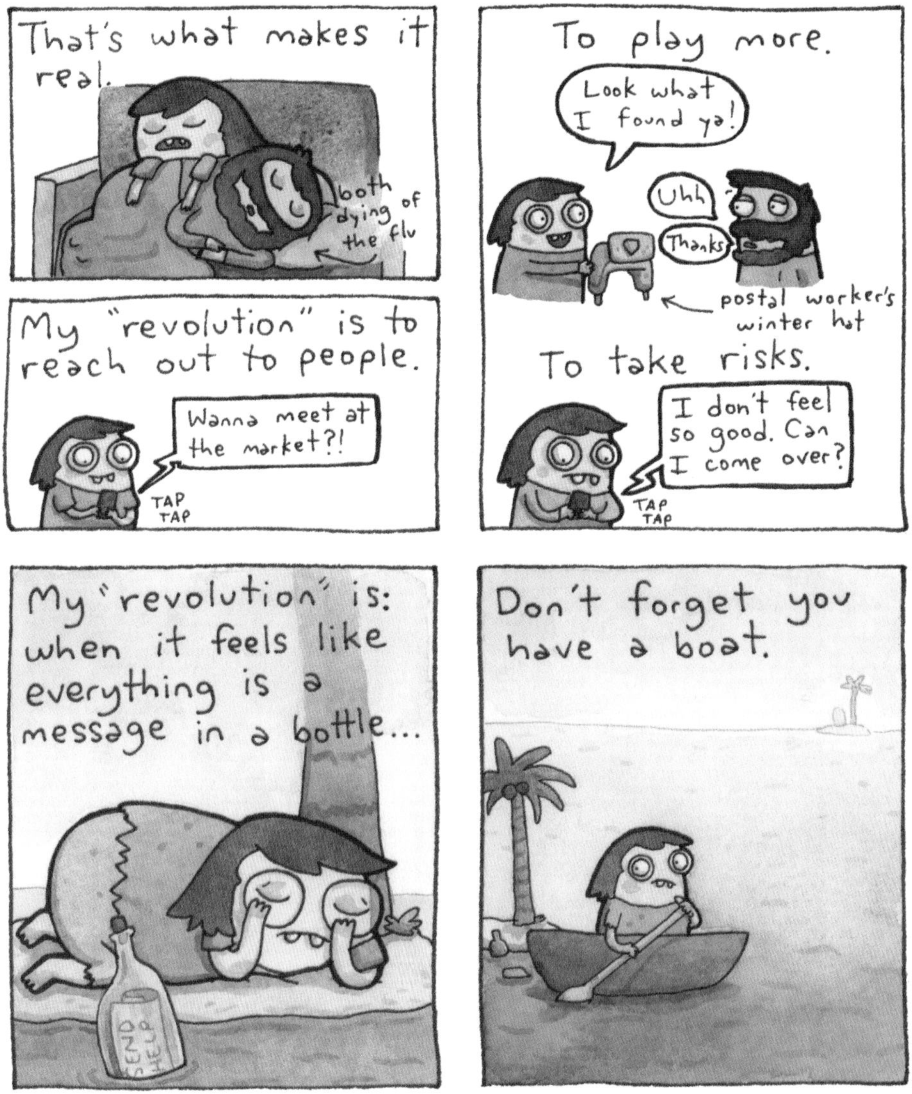
That's what makes it real.
both dying of the flu
My "revolution" is to reach out to people.
Wanna meet at the market?!
TAP TAP
To play more.
Look what I found ya!
Uhh
Thanks
postal worker's winter hat
To take risks.
I don't feel so good. Can I come over?
TAP TAP
My "revolution" is: when it feels like everything is a message in a bottle...
SEND HELP
Don't forget you have a boat.

# Early Childhood Experiments

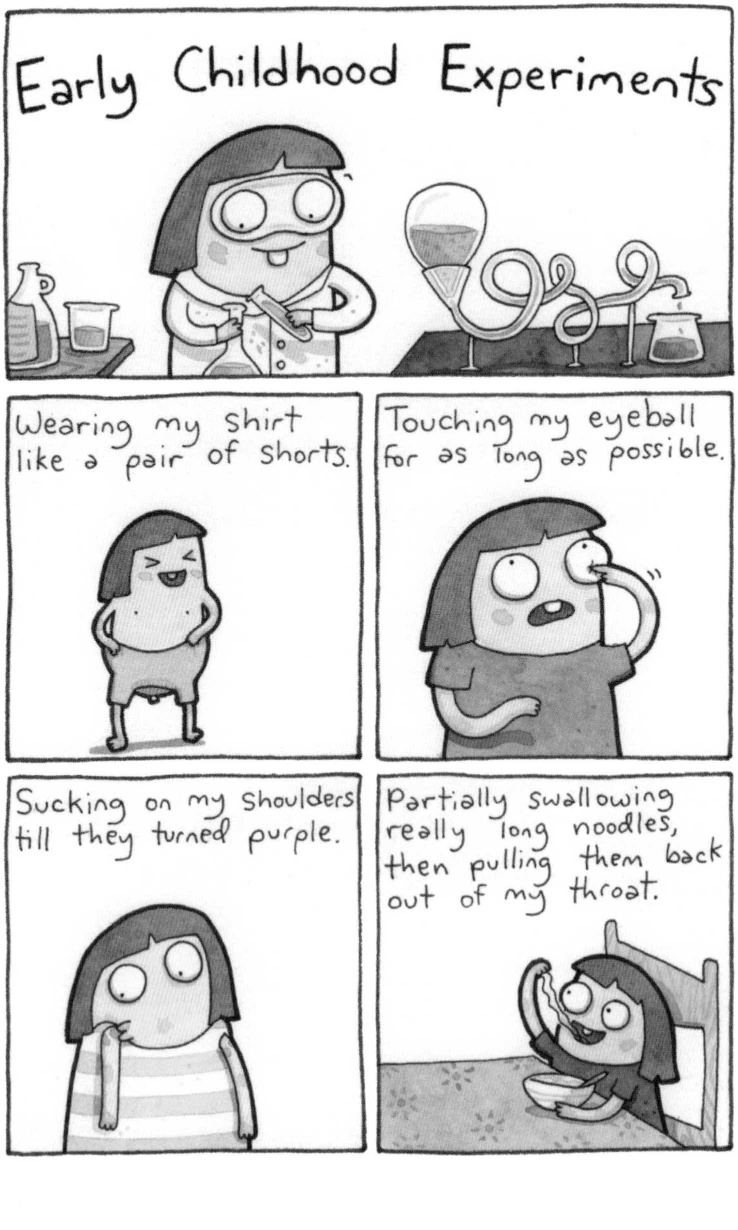
Early Childhood Experiments
Wearing my shirt like a pair of shorts.
Touching my eyeball for as long as possible.
Sucking on my shoulders till they turned purple.
Partially swallowing really long noodles, then pulling them back out of my throat.

Putting my shoes on the wrong feet.

Peeing on the toilet like a boy.

Seeing how shiny I could make a penny by sucking on it.

Sticking my tongue out of my mouth until it dried up.

Staring directly into the sun.

Swallowing a board game piece to see if I could find it later.*

*I couldn't

# Flashlight

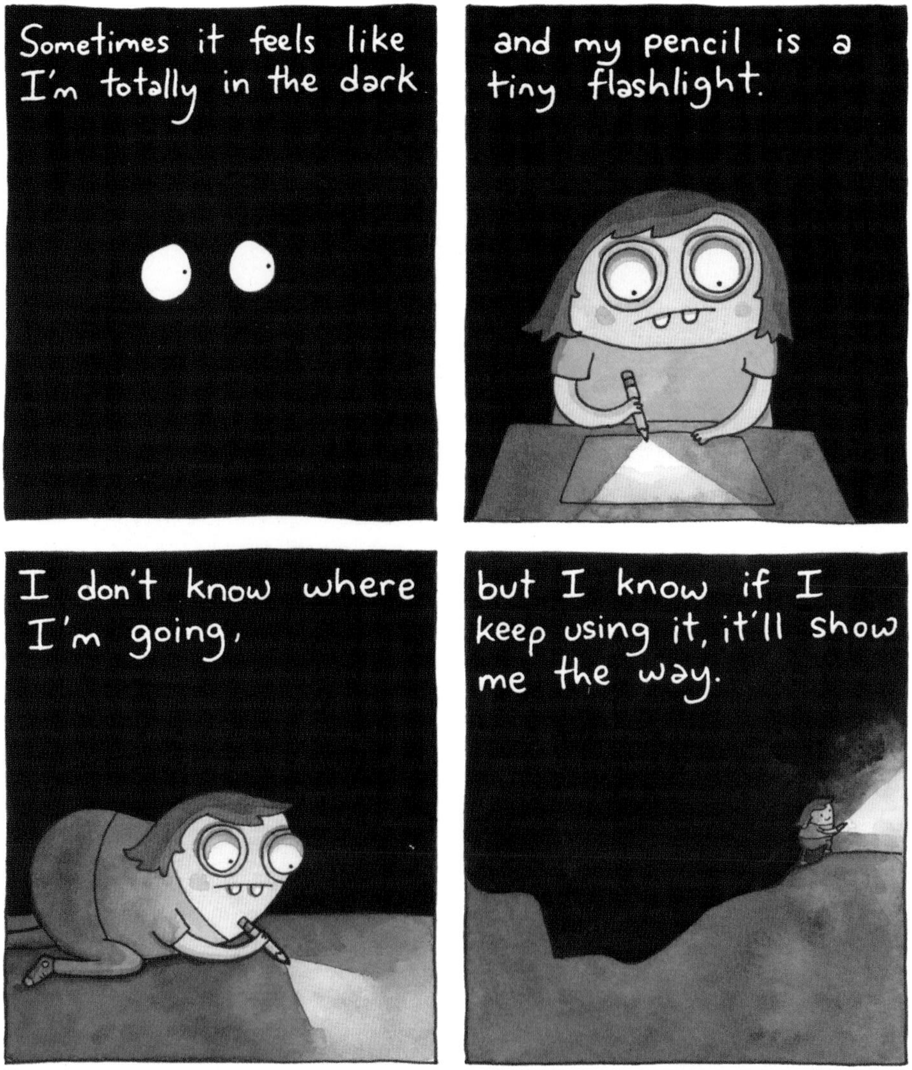
Sometimes it feels like I'm totally in the dark
and my pencil is a tiny flashlight.
I don't know where I'm going,
but I know if I keep using it, it'll show me the way.

# Undies

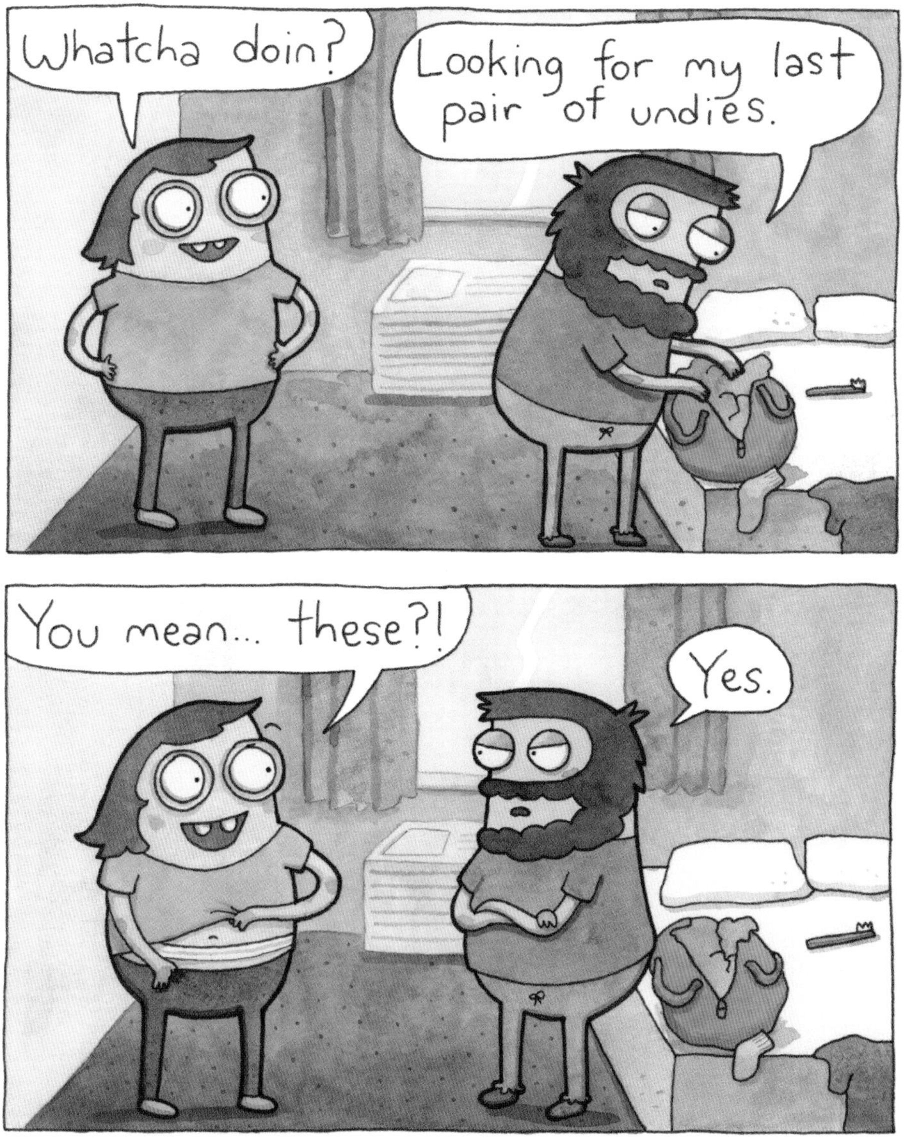
Whatcha doin?
Looking for my last pair of undies.
You mean... these?!
Yes.

# Moving Away

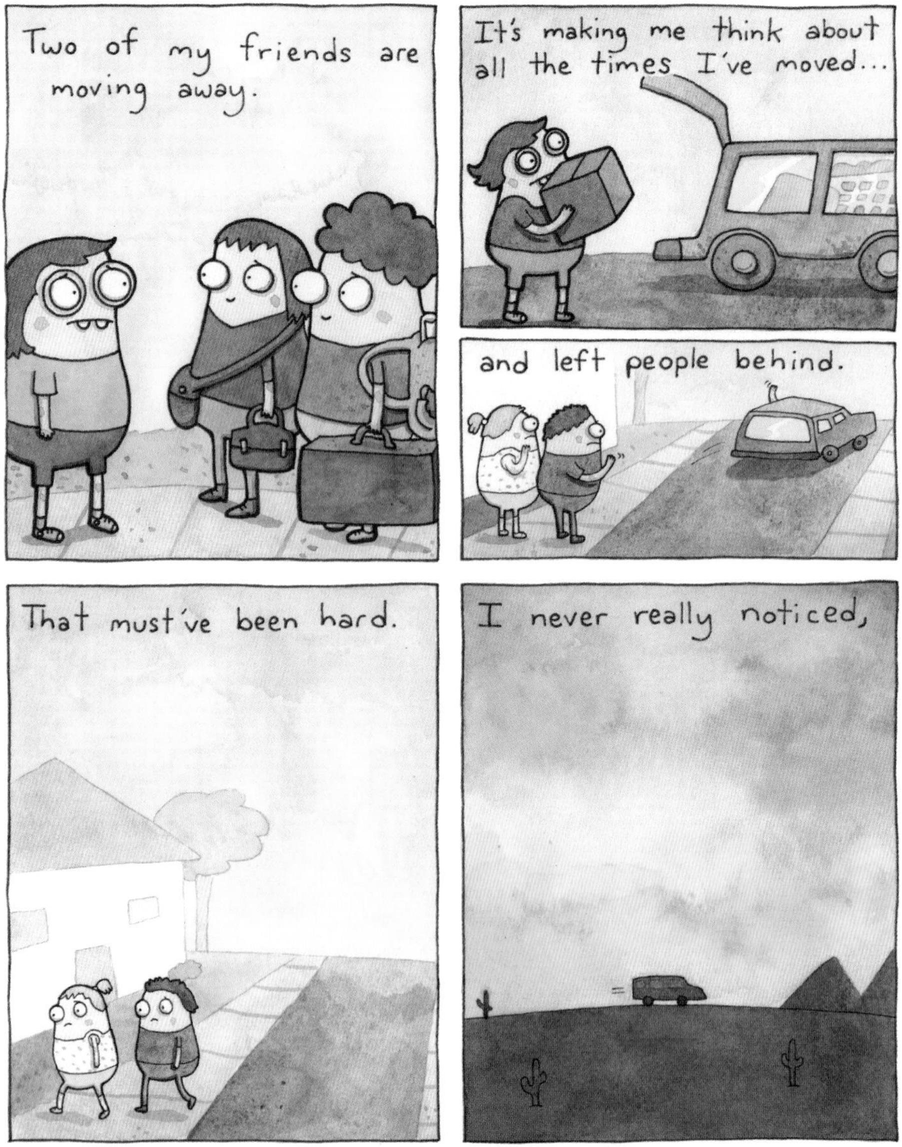
Two of my friends are moving away.
It's making me think about all the times I've moved...
and left people behind.
That must've been hard.
I never really noticed,

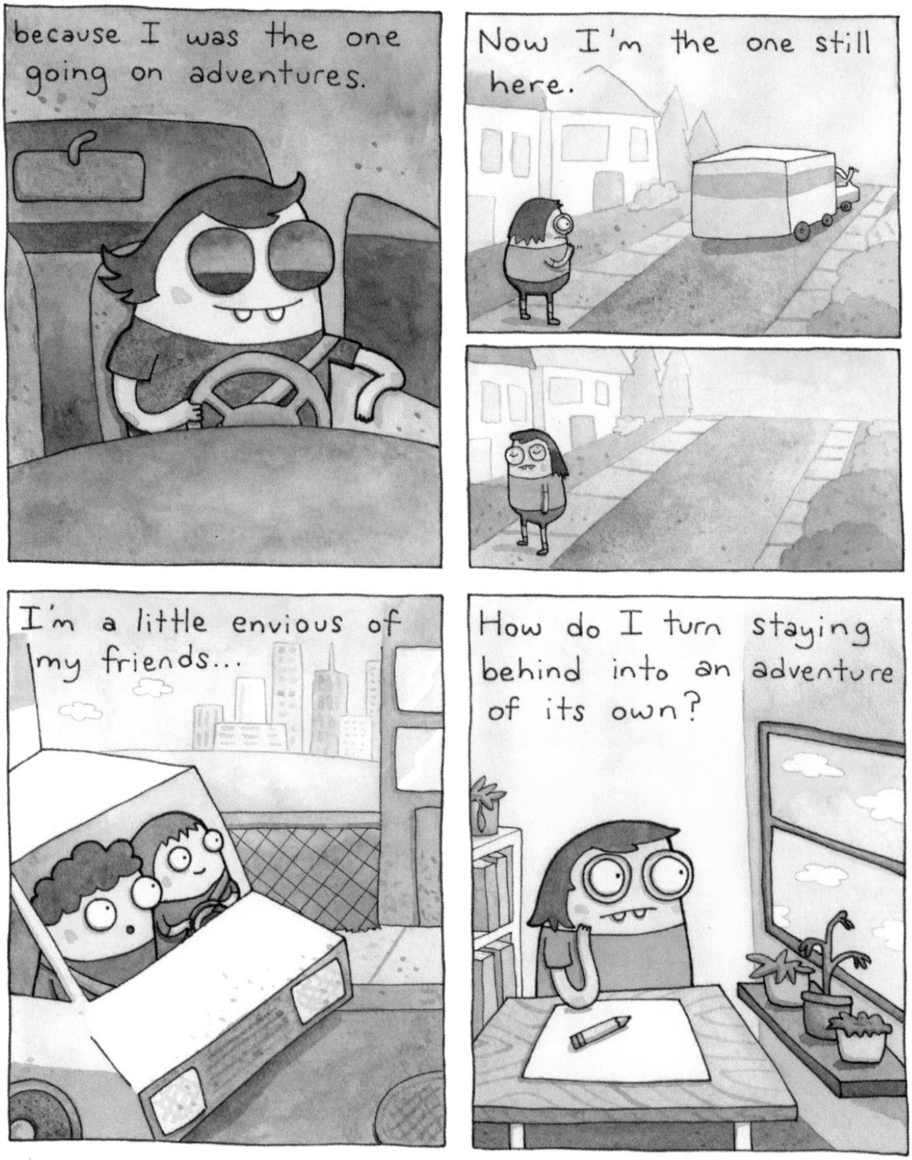
because I was the one going on adventures.
Now I'm the one still here.
I'm a little envious of my friends...
How do I turn staying behind into an adventure of its own?

## Lie to Myself

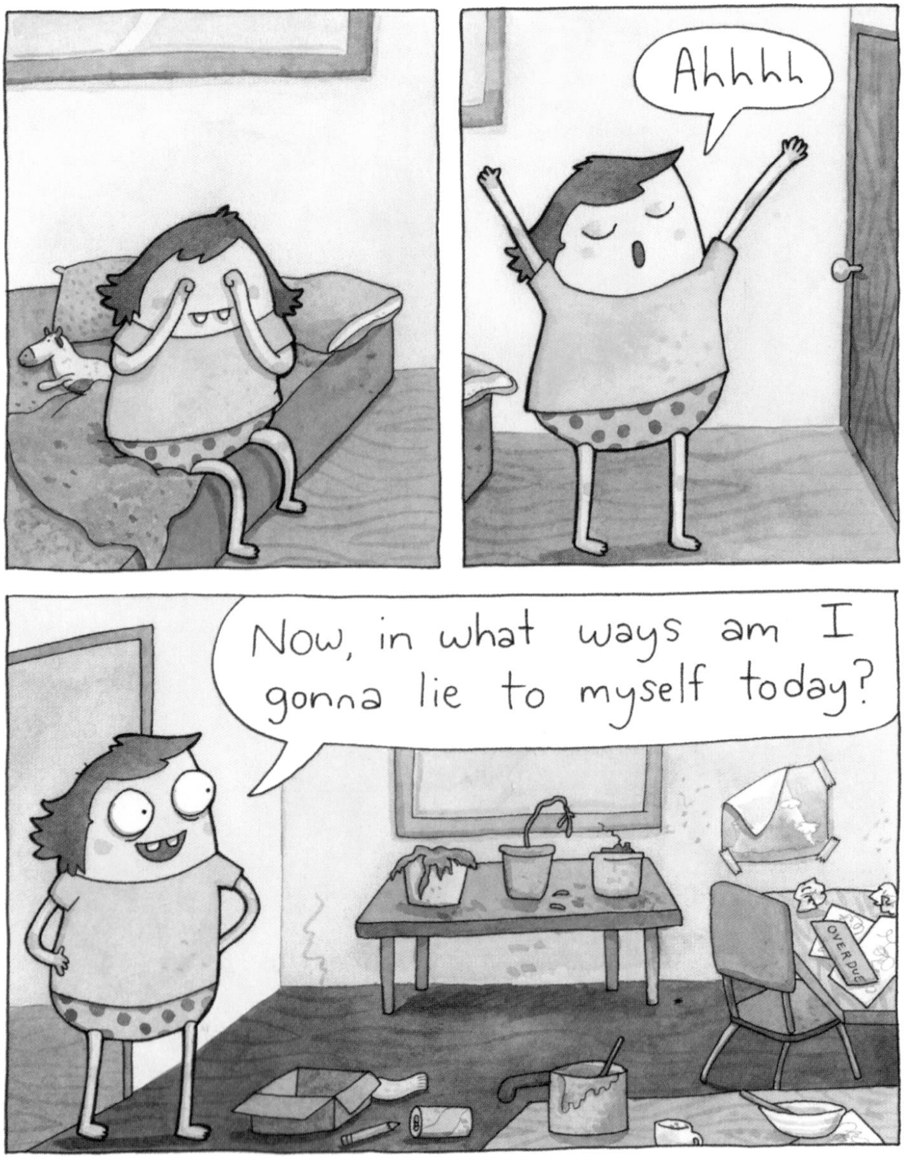
Ahhhh
Now, in what ways am I gonna lie to myself today?
OVERDUE

## Unicorn Shampoo

When I shampoo my hair, I like to lather it into a big soapy point.
And pretend I'm a unicorn.
Rinse, please.
Neigh.

# Jerk

**Panel 1:**

In my early 20s, I was a jerk.

What?! The Beatles can't be your favorite band. They're like everyone's favorite band.

I dunno, I just love them.

**Panel 2:**

I couldn't understand how anyone liked the things I didn't.

I'm sooo excited for the new baseball season!

**Panel 3:**

And I thought if I didn't say exactly what I was thinking, I wasn't being true to who I was.

All they do is stand around and wear tight pants.

**Panel 4:**

When people got offended, which was often, I'd tell myself:

Jeeze, some people just can't handle the truth.

Then I'd continue on with my dangerous combination of extreme opinions and a compulsion to share them.
I could never work in a cubicle.
You actually like going to the mall?
But why would you wear a sweater without sleeves?
I suspect this cost me a lot of things... like jobs
Hey, you forgot to put me on the schedule next week.
Yeahhh about that...
...and invitations
Can't wait to meet your parents!
Umm... we'll see.
... and my sanity.
why does everyone suck but me?!

One night, in a moment of desperation, I turned to the Internet for reassurance
Why does everyone suck but me?
but it just told me what I'd really known all along.
Maybe it's you?

Sometimes you don't have to do anything.
It's okay to just...
beeeee
Unless it's winter, of course.
Then ya gotta bundle up.

There's this voice in my head that tells me I'm never good enough.

It tells me other people are the <u>only</u> reason I got where I am.

It makes me desperately seek approval.

Sooo waddaya think?!

Hmm, this might work.

It makes me doubt myself.

Nah, it probably stinks.

It tells me I'm stupid all the time.

I'm sick of this voice.

Leave me alone!

I'm going to try something new.

Hmm

Brave for taking chances.

Let's do this thing.

Brave for making mistakes!

Every time I notice the voice telling me I'm stupid...

I - I...

I'm going to try telling myself I'm actually <u>brave</u>.

Brave for believing in myself.

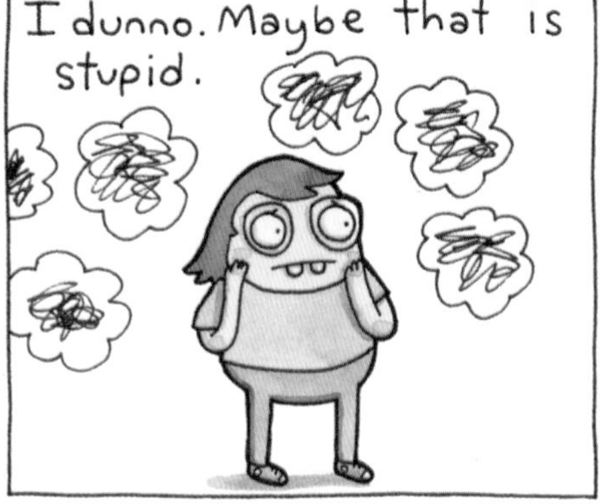
I dunno. Maybe that is stupid.

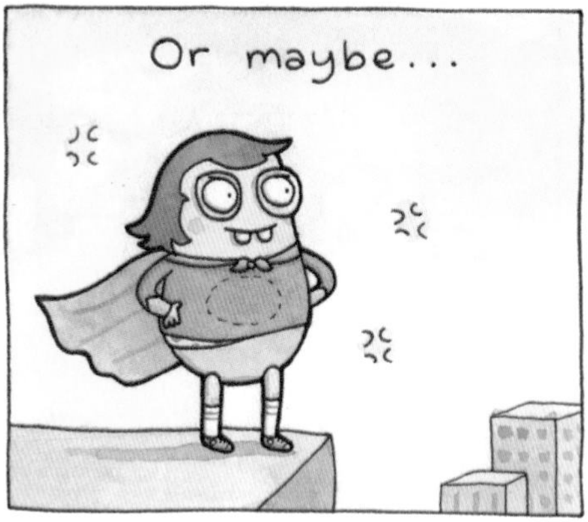
Or maybe...

## Ball Pit

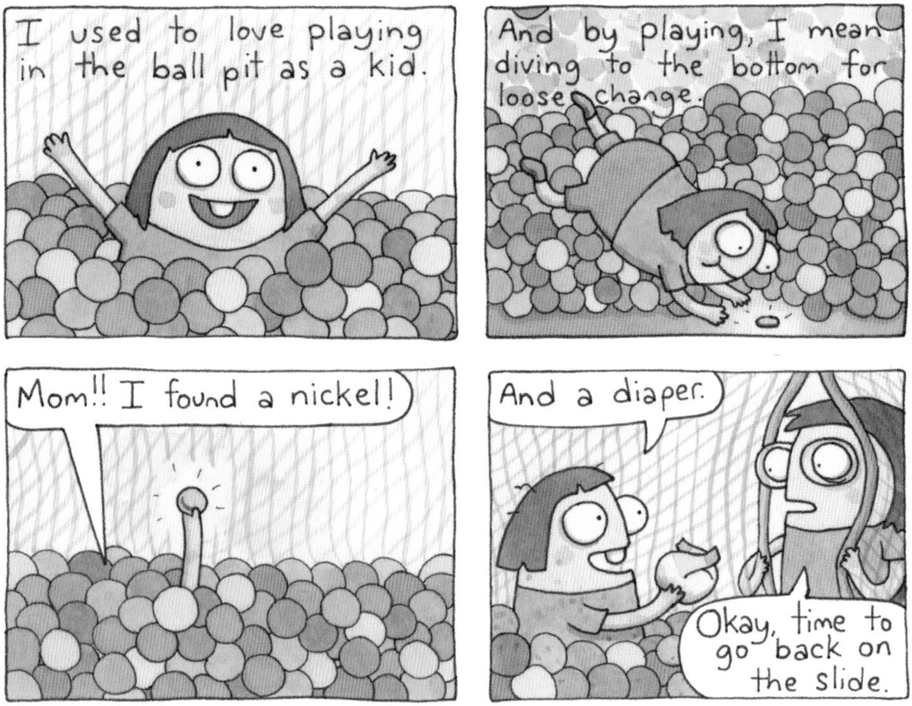
I used to love playing in the ball pit as a kid.
And by playing, I mean diving to the bottom for loose change.
Mom!! I found a nickel!
And a diaper.
Okay, time to go back on the slide.

My grandpa lived in the Veteran's Hospital for a long time.

He'd had a stroke and couldn't really talk.

Hrmph.

But he managed to interact in different ways. Like painting ceramic figurines in the craft room,

playing games after lunch

Bingo!

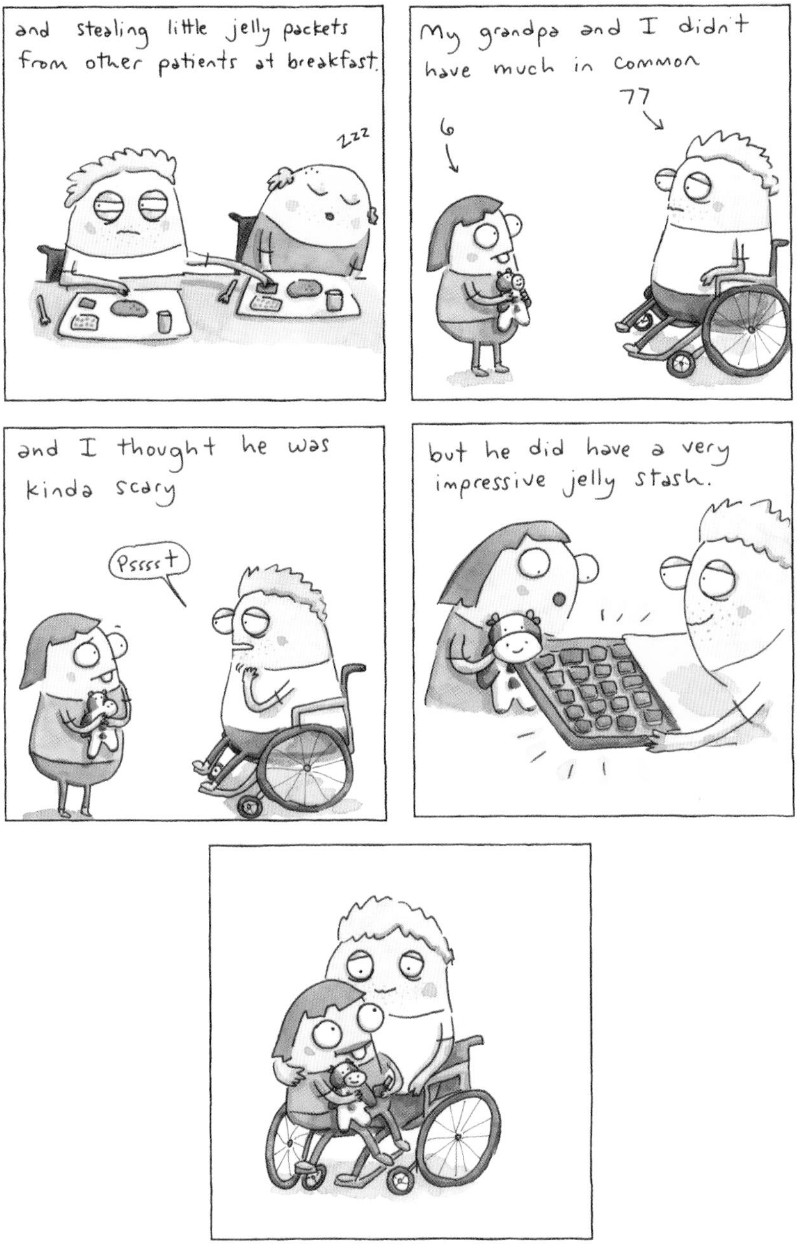
and stealing little jelly packets from other patients at breakfast.
zzz
My grandpa and I didn't have much in common
6
77
and I thought he was kinda scary
Psssst
but he did have a very impressive jelly stash.

Afraid

I've always loved doing things for other people
Can I clean your room?
Uhh okay.
even if they could do it themselves.
Oh man, I'm gonna have to pull an all-nighter.
I'll stay up with ya!

I used to think it was out of love.
Already made dinner!
But it was actually out of fear.
Need a ride later?!
Not really, but umm sure.

I was afraid if I wasn't useful, people wouldn't need me anymore.

Just cleaned the whole apartment!

Uh coooo.

Or that my regular old self wasn't enough.

You're gonna take a cab? No way! I love getting up at 3am.

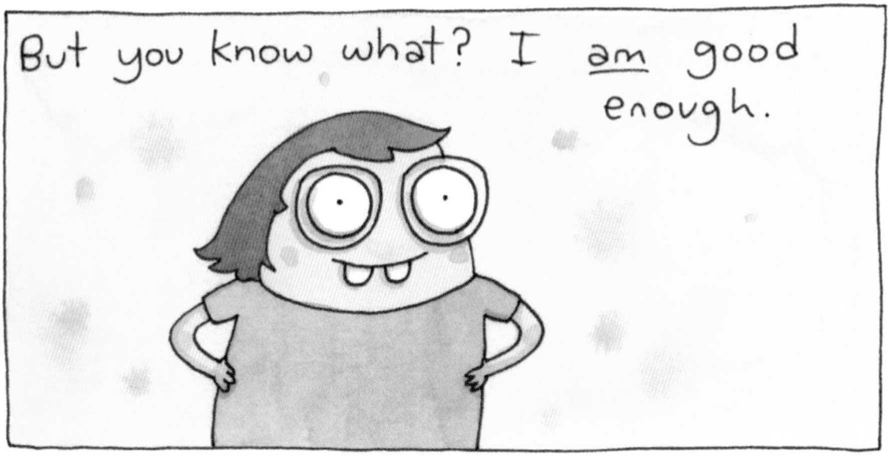
But you know what? I am good enough.

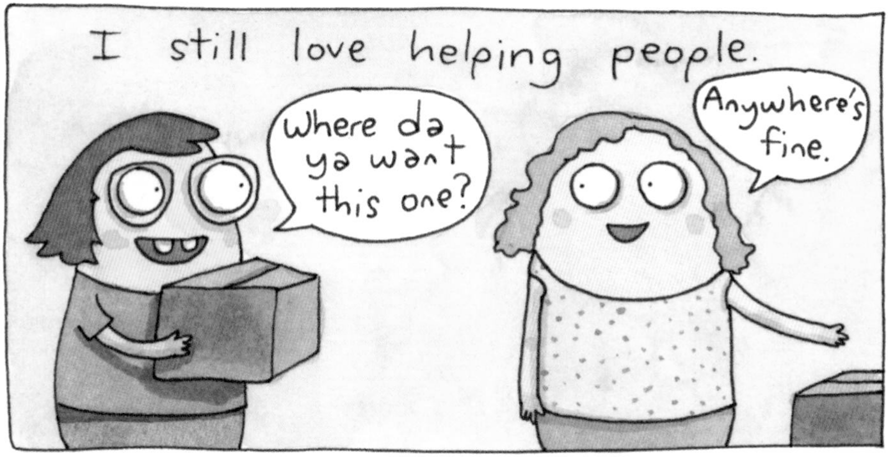
I still love helping people.
Where da ya want this one?
Anywhere's fine.

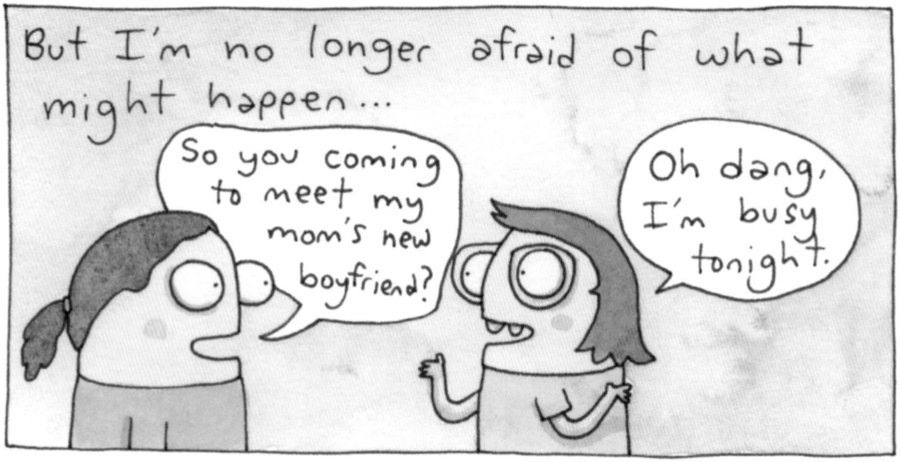
But I'm no longer afraid of what might happen...
So you coming to meet my mom's new boyfriend?
Oh dang, I'm busy tonight.

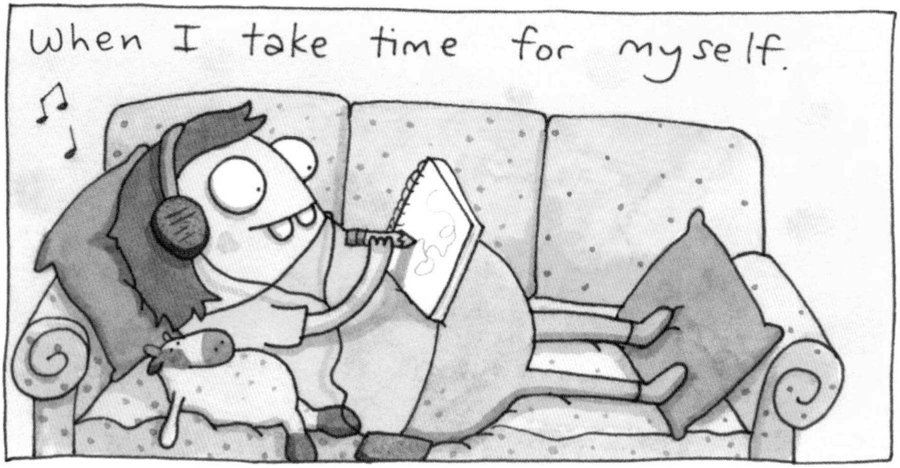
When I take time for myself.

I keep waiting for permission.

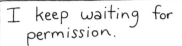

Permission to try something new.

Permission to take risks

Even permission to make mistakes

It's like I'm in line waiting for someone to say

Okay, kid. You're up.

But the longer I wait

the more I wonder

What if the only person that can really grant me permission...

is me?

## Autocorrect

Man, I HATE Spellcheck!
I think you mean Autocorrect.

# Look Like This Forever

What if I look like this forever?
I'll still love ya.
I don't care how you look.
I just care how you feel.
Really?!

# Lemonade

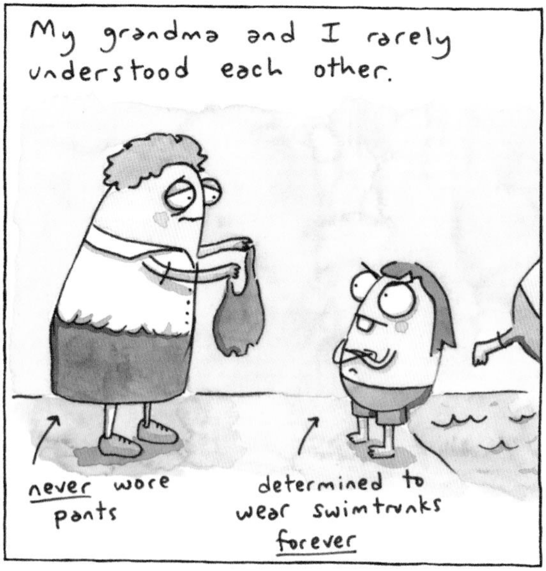
My grandma and I rarely understood each other.
never wore pants
determined to wear swimtrunks forever

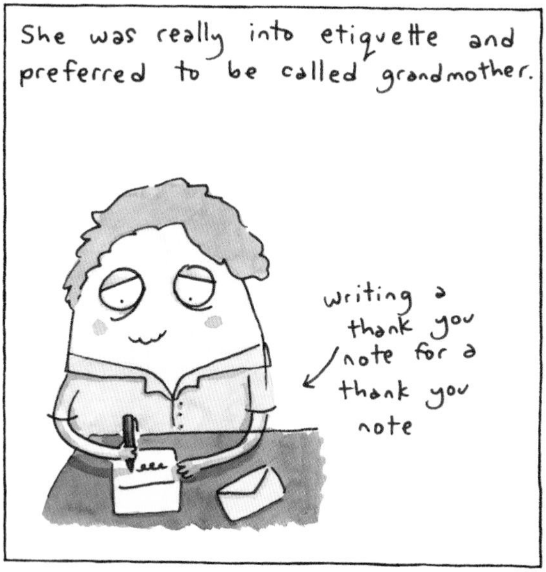
She was really into etiquette and preferred to be called grandmother.
writing a thank you note for a thank you note

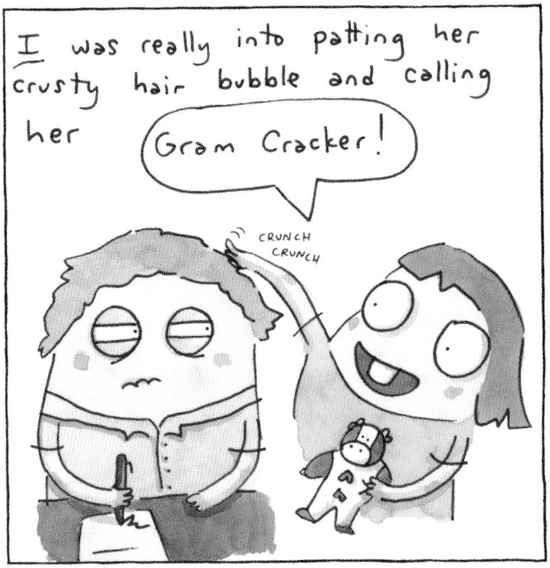
I was really into patting her crusty hair bubble and calling her
Gram Cracker!
CRUNCH CRUNCH

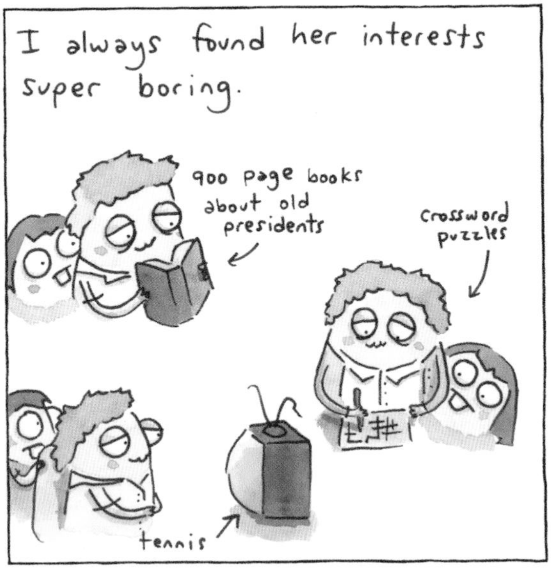
I always found her interests super boring.
900 page books about old presidents
crossword puzzles
tennis

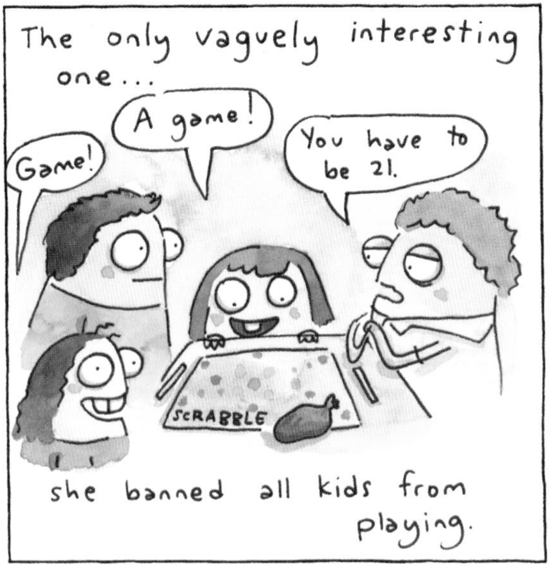
The only vaguely interesting one...
Game!
A game!
You have to be 21.
SCRABBLE
she banned all kids from playing.

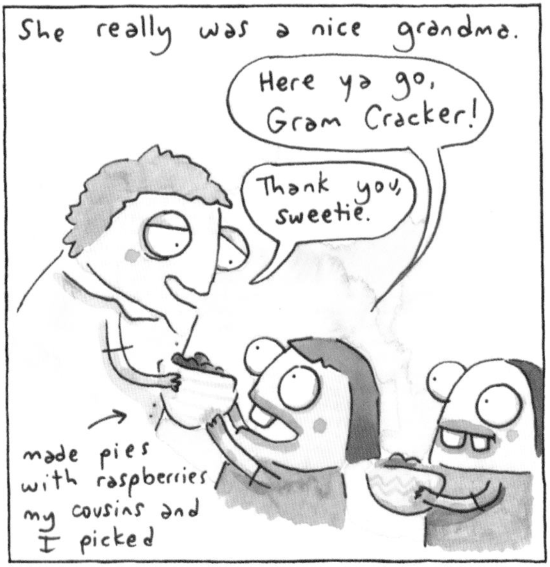
She really was a nice grandma.
Here ya go, Gram Cracker!
Thank you, sweetie.
made pies with raspberries my cousins and I picked

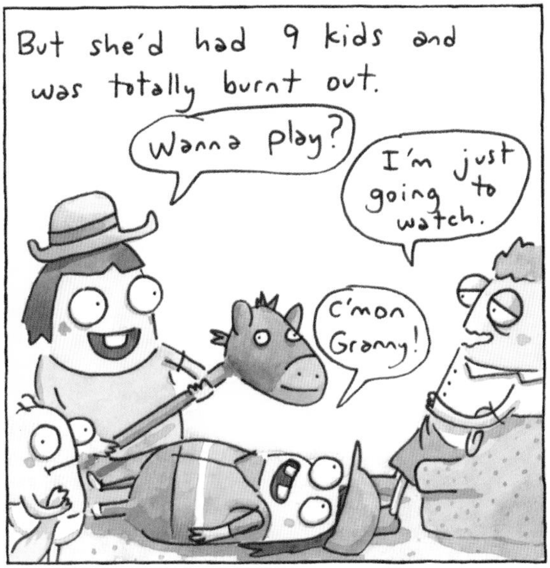
But she'd had 9 kids and was totally burnt out.
Wanna play?
I'm just going to watch.
C'mon Granny!

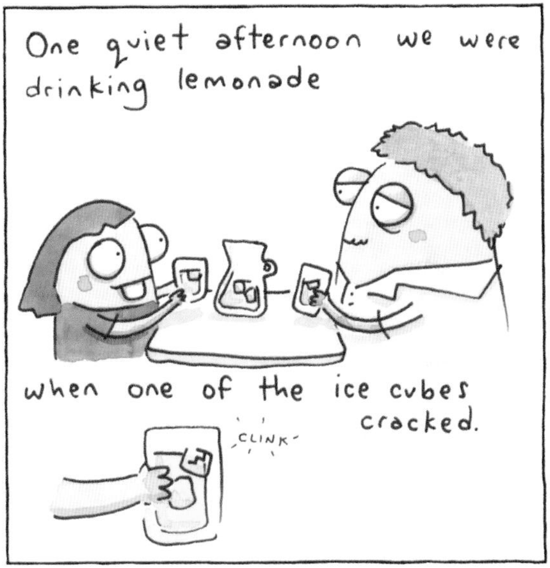
One quiet afternoon we were drinking lemonade
when one of the ice cubes cracked.
CLINK

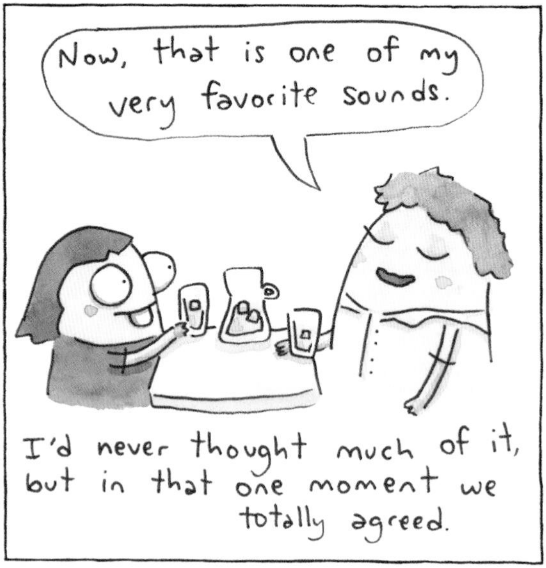
Now, that is one of my very favorite sounds.
I'd never thought much of it, but in that one moment we totally agreed.

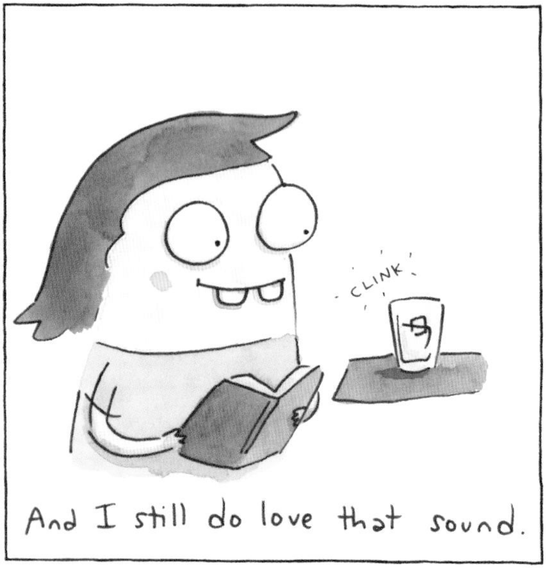
CLINK
And I still do love that sound.

# Plushies

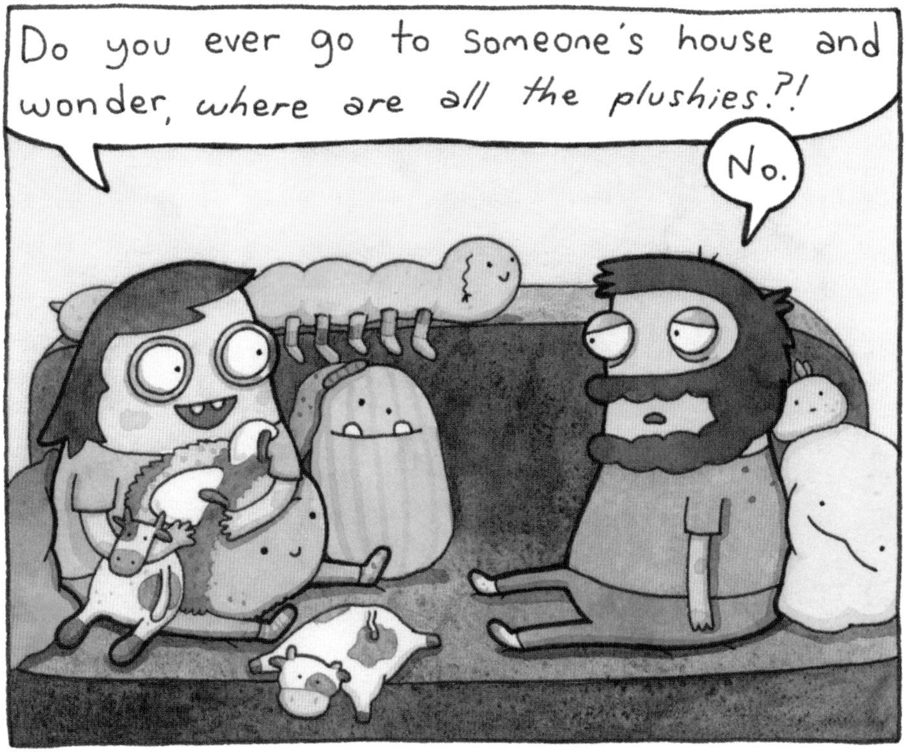

Do you ever go to someone's house and wonder, where are all the plushies?!
No.

I feel like there's a door opening inside me.

And this warm beautiful breeze is blowing in.

For a long time I kept the door closed.

I was so afraid of all the bad getting in,

I didn't realize how much bad needed to get out.

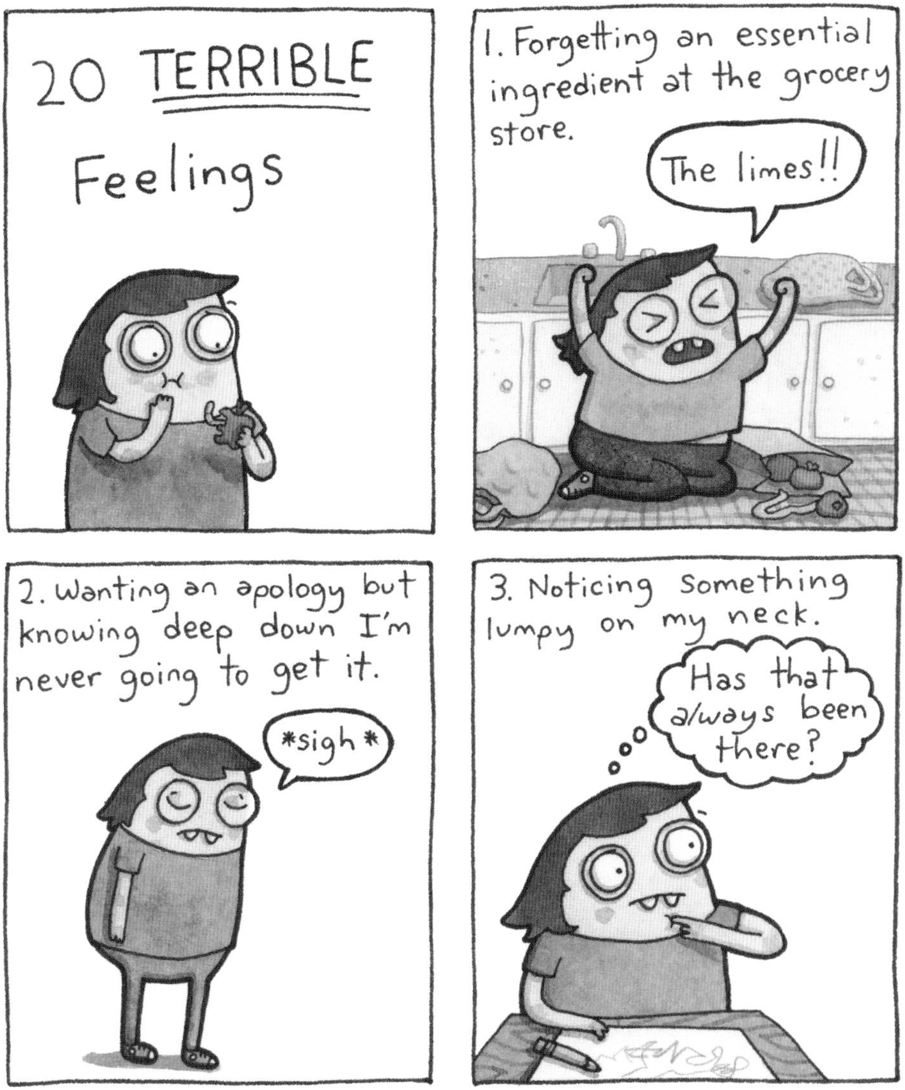
20 TERRIBLE Feelings
1. Forgetting an essential ingredient at the grocery store.
The limes!!
2. Wanting an apology but knowing deep down I'm never going to get it.
*sigh*
3. Noticing something lumpy on my neck.
Has that always been there?

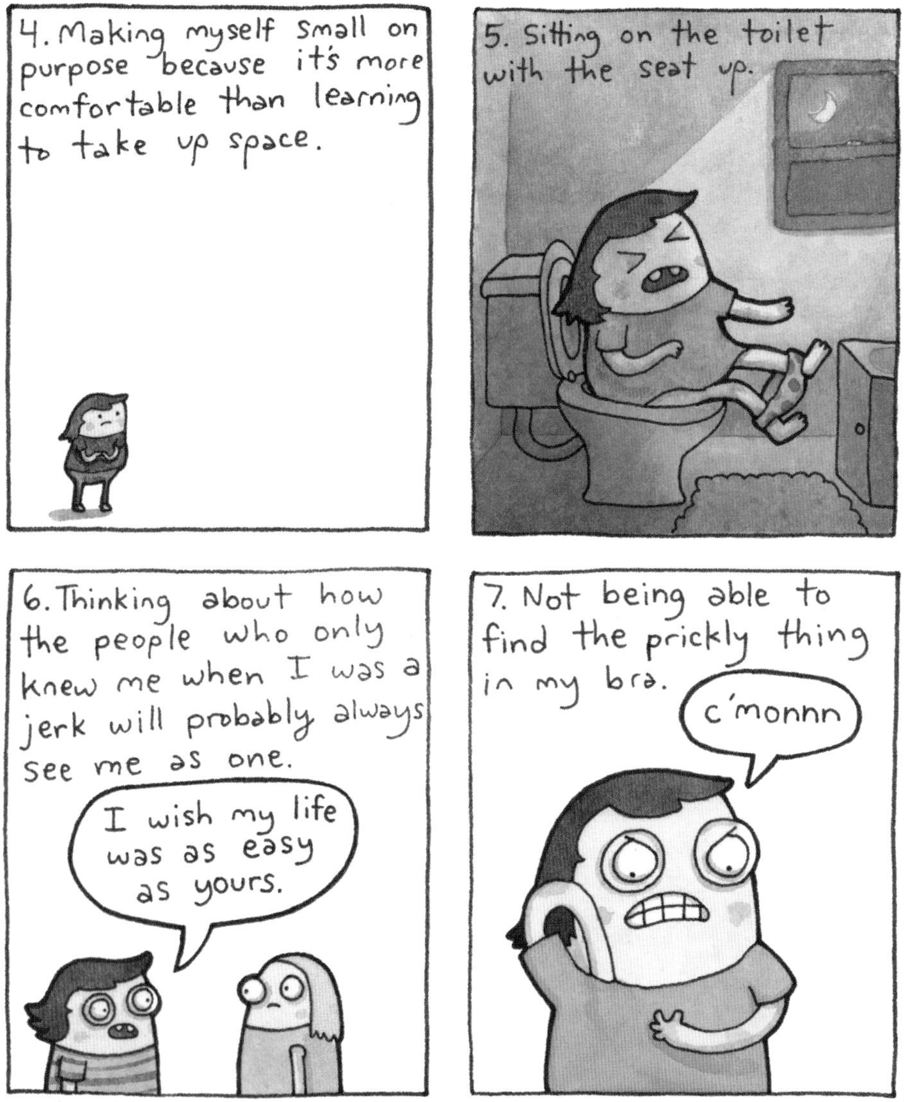
4. Making myself small on purpose because it's more comfortable than learning to take up space.
5. Sitting on the toilet with the seat up.
6. Thinking about how the people who only knew me when I was a jerk will probably always see me as one.
I wish my life was as easy as yours.
7. Not being able to find the prickly thing in my bra.
c'monnn

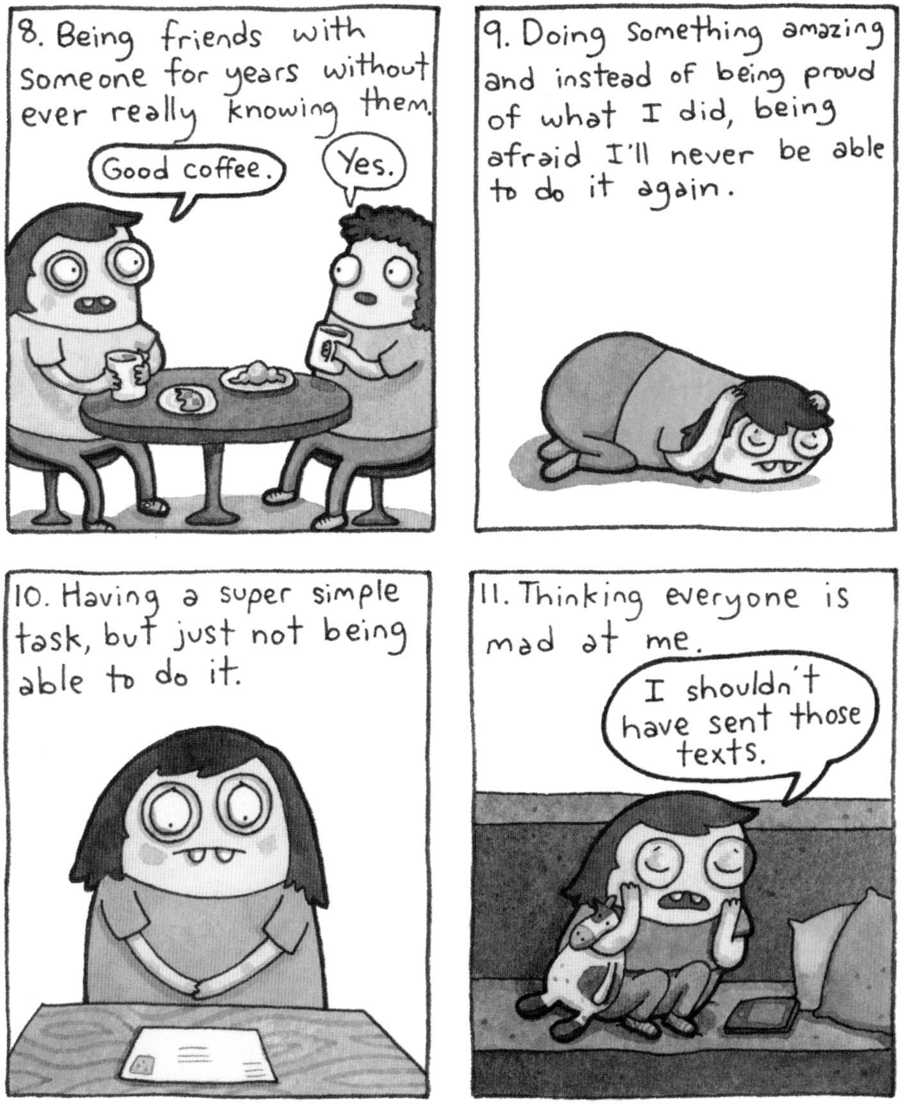
8. Being friends with someone for years without ever really knowing them.
Good coffee.
Yes.
9. Doing something amazing and instead of being proud of what I did, being afraid I'll never be able to do it again.
10. Having a super simple task, but just not being able to do it.
11. Thinking everyone is mad at me.
I shouldn't have sent those texts.

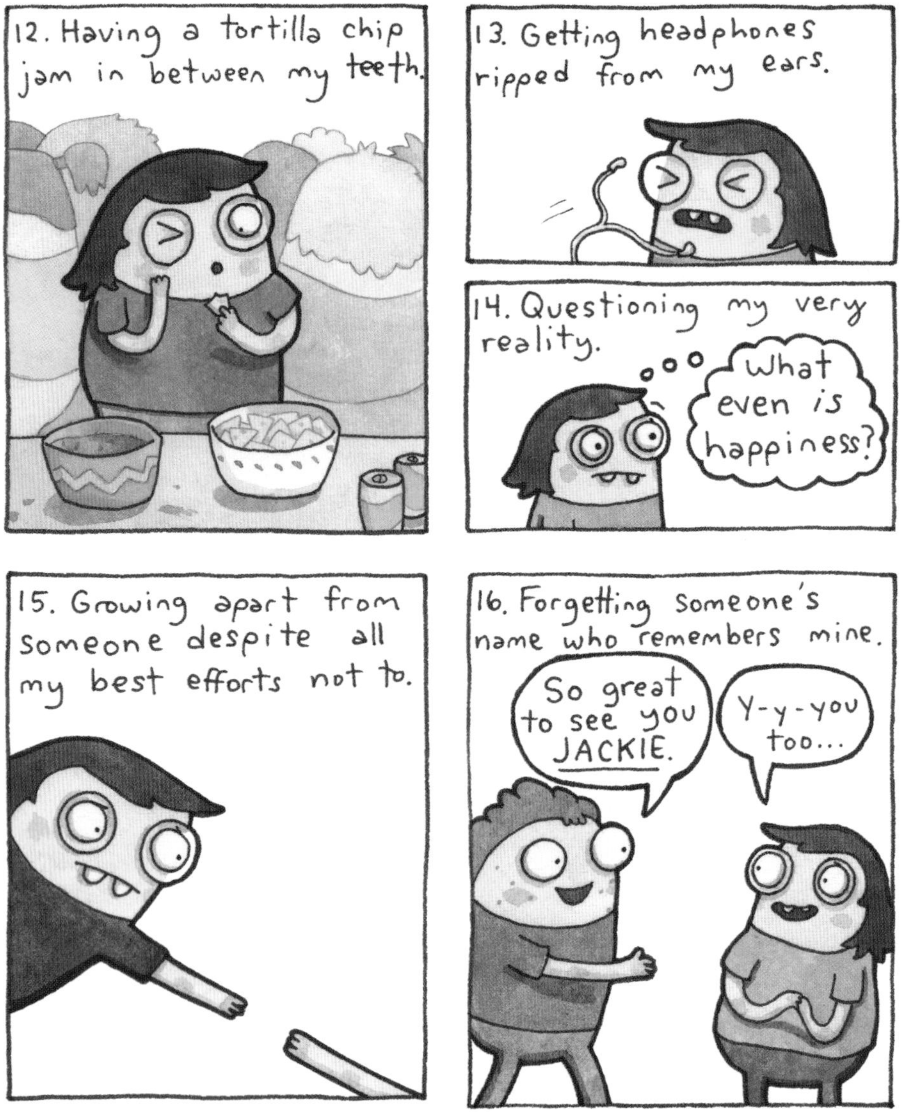
12. Having a tortilla chip jam in between my teeth.
13. Getting headphones ripped from my ears.
14. Questioning my very reality.
What even is happiness?
15. Growing apart from someone despite all my best efforts not to.
16. Forgetting someone's name who remembers mine.
So great to see you JACKIE.
Y-y-you too...

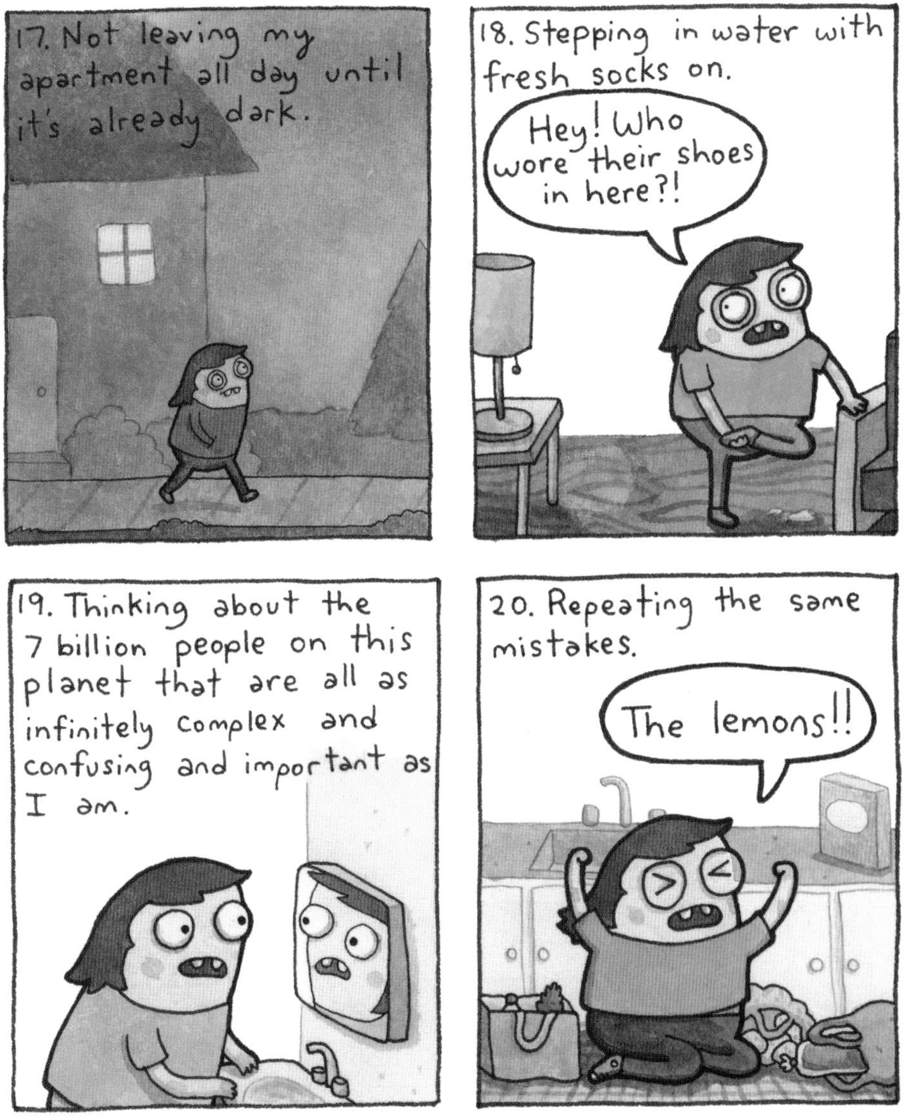
17. Not leaving my apartment all day until it's already dark.
18. Stepping in water with fresh socks on.
Hey! Who wore their shoes in here?!
19. Thinking about the 7 billion people on this planet that are all as infinitely complex and confusing and important as I am.
20. Repeating the same mistakes.
The lemons!!

## Can't Sleep

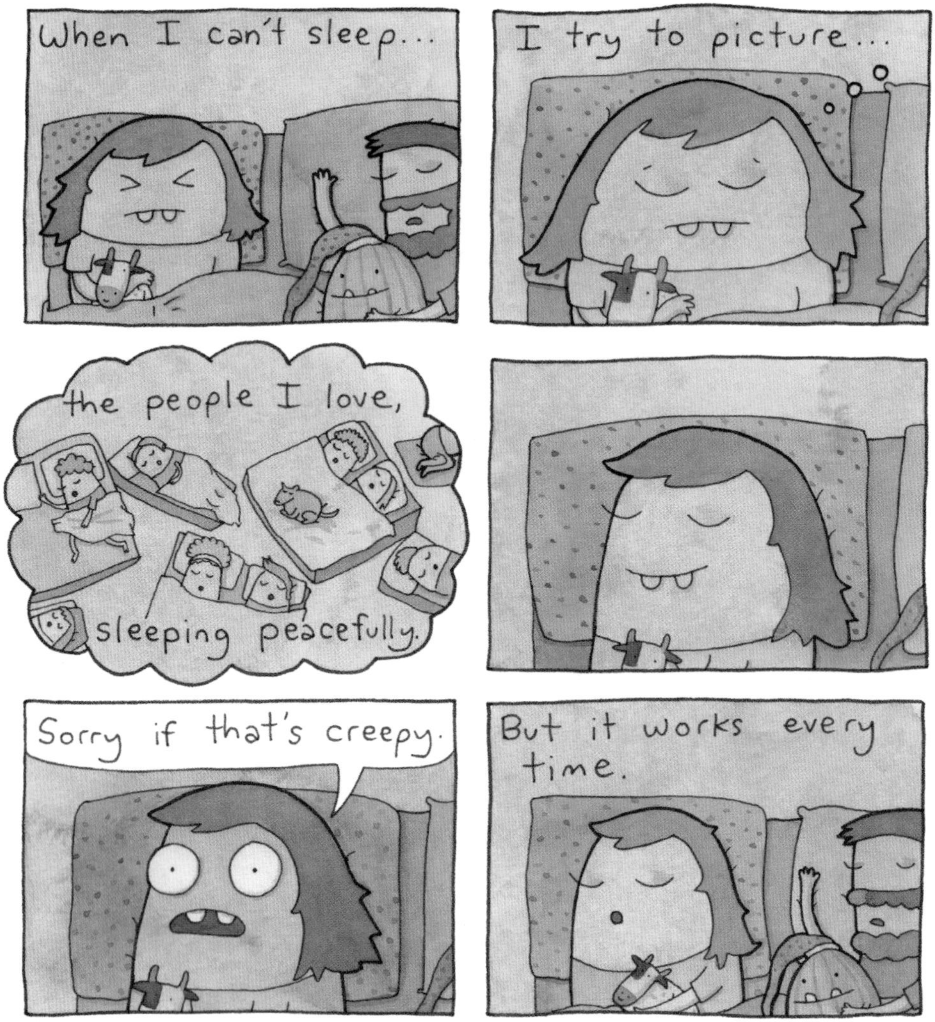
When I can't sleep...
I try to picture...
the people I love,
sleeping peacefully.
Sorry if that's creepy.
But it works every time.

I LOVE seeing laundry hanging out to dry.

There's something so human about it. So... uniting.

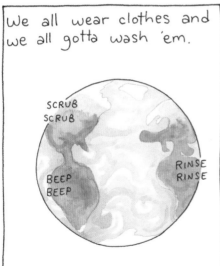

We all wear clothes and we all gotta wash 'em.

SCRUB
SCRUB

BEEP
BEEP

RINSE
RINSE

Laundry is the flag waved by all humanity.

# Marriage

I didn't think marriage would feel any different from dating.

Till death do you part?

Uhh sure, why not?

In a lot of ways it's the same.

still the little spoon

still addicted to bagels

still need alone time

Hissssss

But something about marriage is different. *

* aside from our cool matching rings that is

When we were dating, our relationship was like a rental property.

Uhh the sink's clogged again.

It'll drain eventually.

We did our best to ignore the things that needed work.

But now, we own the house.

I think we better open it.

*gulp

UNRESOLVED ISSUES

Honk

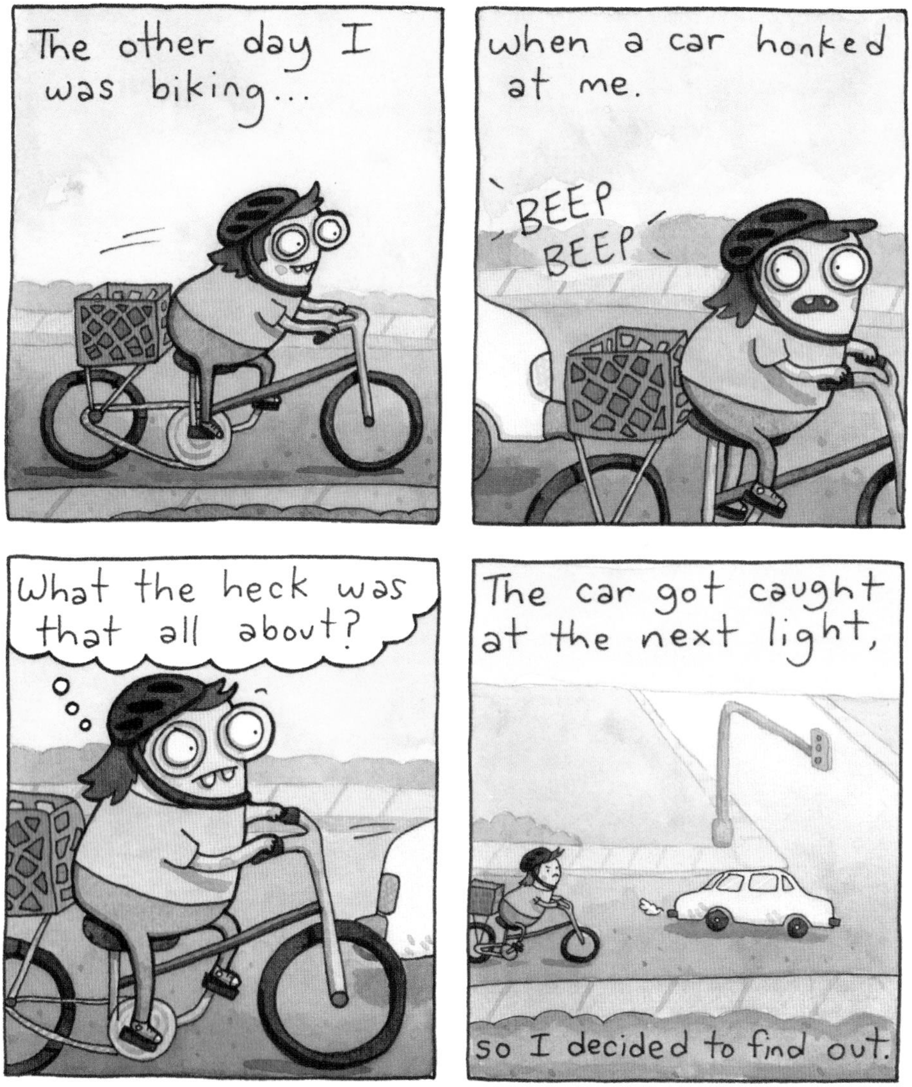
The other day I was biking...
when a car honked at me.
BEEP BEEP
What the heck was that all about?
The car got caught at the next light,
so I decided to find out.

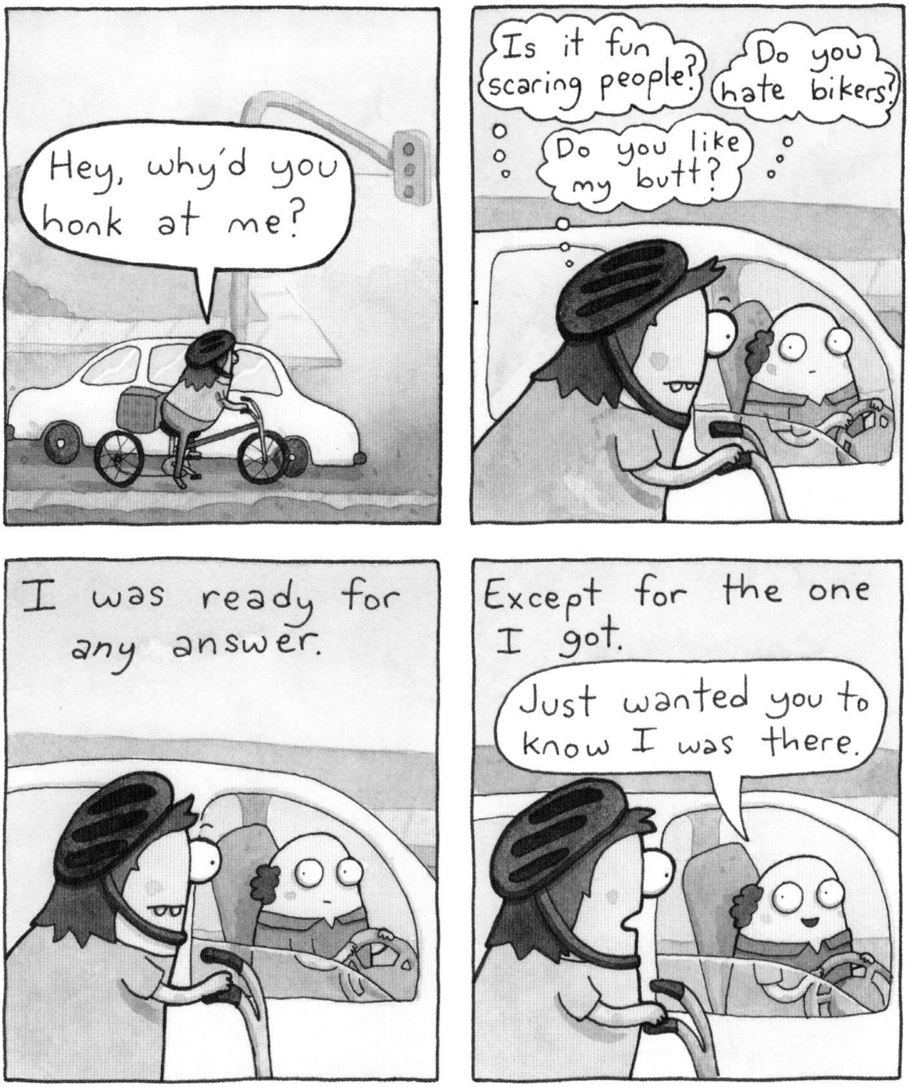
Hey, why'd you honk at me?
Is it fun scaring people?
Do you hate bikers?
Do you like my butt?
I was ready for any answer.
Except for the one I got.
Just wanted you to know I was there.

# Mushroom Hunting

Yesterday in the park...
mm hmm?
...I saw these *beautiful* mushrooms.
I leaned in to get a closer look...
Cheetos

# Tantrum

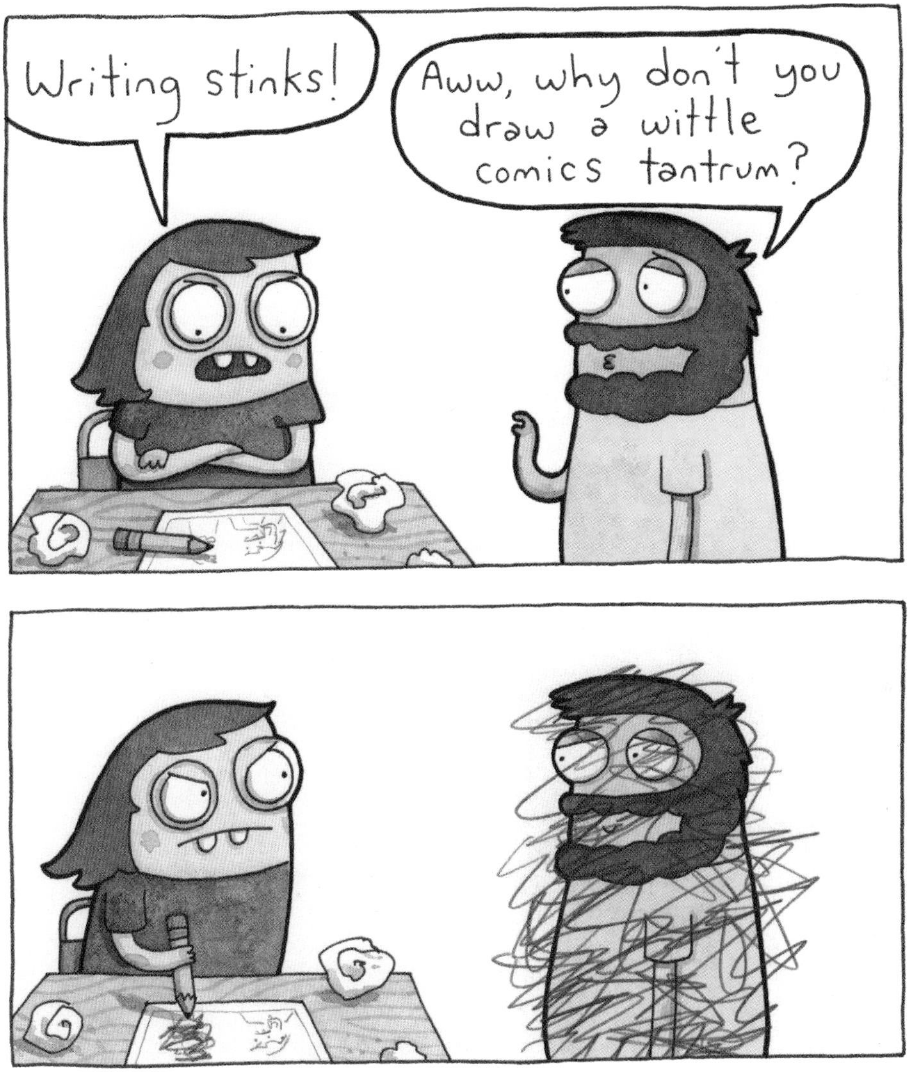
Writing stinks!
Aww, why don't you draw a wittle comics tantrum?

I used to set my alarm clock to a different weird time every night...

CLICK
CLICK
CLICK

because I thought the less popular numbers might feel left out.

Catch ya tomorrow, 7:03.

I just wanted them to know someone was thinking of them.

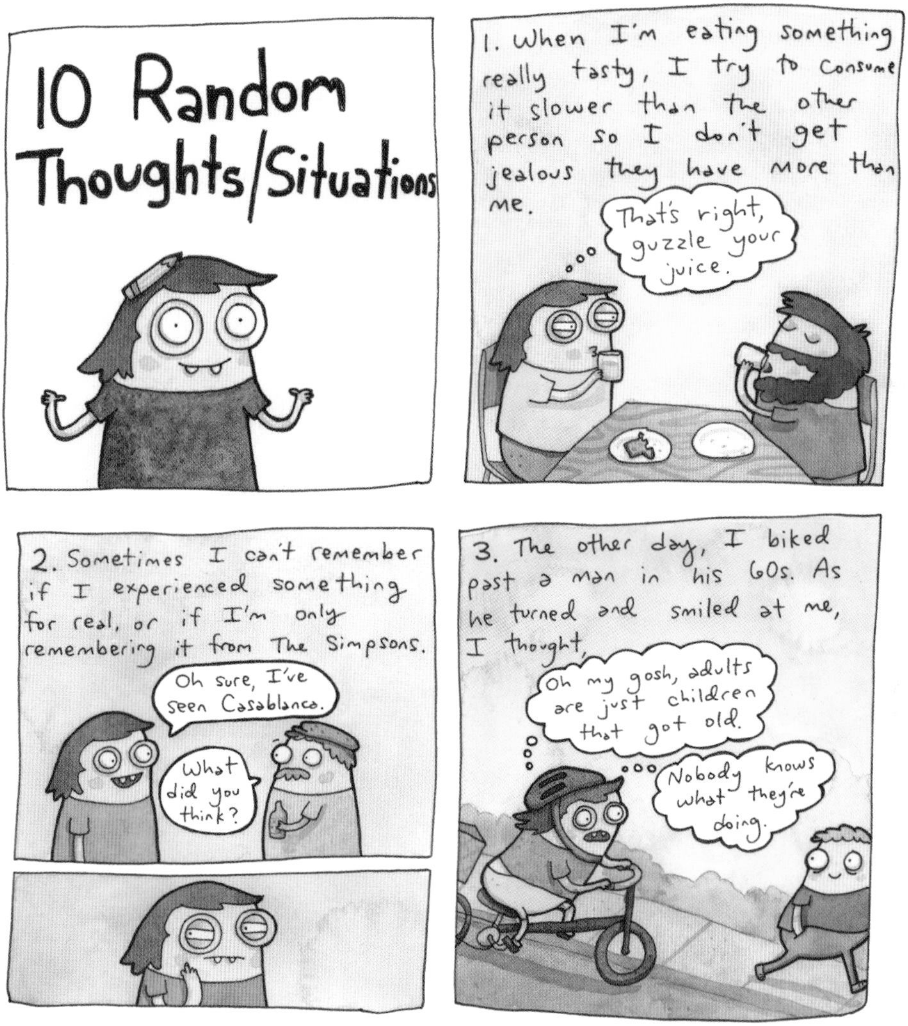
10 Random Thoughts/Situations
1. When I'm eating something really tasty, I try to consume it slower than the other person so I don't get jealous they have more than me.
That's right, guzzle your juice.
2. Sometimes I can't remember if I experienced something for real, or if I'm only remembering it from The Simpsons.
Oh sure, I've seen Casablanca.
What did you think?
3. The other day, I biked past a man in his 60s. As he turned and smiled at me, I thought,
Oh my gosh, adults are just children that got old.
Nobody knows what they're doing.

**4.**

*mmm croutons, the chips of the salad.*

*mmm cereal, the chips of breakfast.*

*mmm, chips.*

**5.**

Maybe I'm so smart that I'm not afraid of looking stupid.

Yeahhh, maybe.

**6.**

Wanna see my new experiment?

Sure.

**7.**

Watch out!

You almost squished a snail.

We gotcha buddy.

Aww, you love all creatures, big and small.

But especially small.

8.
How's my forehead?
Big and smooth.
I meant temperature.

9. Sometimes I like to bypass the thing everyone tells me to look at,
and decide for myself what's beautiful.

10.
Oh, a hair dryer!
I know you've been wanting one.
Thanks.
You get this at a thrift store?
Just enjoy it.

# Couch

I love the way you smell.
What do I smell like?
Hmm...
It's really cozy.
Like...
Like...
A couch!
A really clean couch.

The harder I try to make something perfect...

the more it seems to fall apart.

So I'm starting to wonder...

what good is "perfect" anyway

when there's so much beauty in mistakes?

# Minivan Voyage

Minivan Voyage
When I was 19, I went with my cousin and her friends on a road trip to Montreal.
She was a year younger than me, but everyone considered her to be the more responsible one (and still does).
I'd been living with my cousin and her family all summer and it felt like pure freedom.
I had my own bike.
My own room.
And my own money.

I'd gotten a part-time job off Craigslist designing a website for two women starting some kind of t-shirt vending machine company.
You ever done this before?
No, but I like to draw and go on the Internet a lot.
You're hired!
I did some work, but mostly I sat alone in their rented office space watching movies and intermittently doing crunches.
When I wasn't "working" I was...
Watching horror movies with my youngest cousin
Crashing the community pool
Picking up lucrative babysitting gigs
I can't thank you enough.
Oh, anytime.
and eating double fudge dollar sundaes in suburban parking lots at night.

That summer had everything.

Well, everything except boys.

They had to have been around somewhere,

but the only ones I could find were either...

my friends' older or younger brothers.

Nothing in between.

I didn't have much luck with boys even when they were around.

So... wanna come over later?

Hold up, lemme rescue this worm.

I'd kissed one once,

Squishy

Shared a hookah pipe with another,

His mouth touched this!

and got danced on by one at a frat party, but that definitely wasn't what I wanted.

Eek!

← luckily I'd worn a backpack

What I really wanted was to feel something magical I hadn't before.

89

As we crossed the border into Canada I decided...

°°° I'm gonna kiss a Montreal boy!

Maybe I'd just been in the wrong country all this time!

I think everyone in the van had the same idea because as soon as we parked at our hostel, we set out to find a bar.

So cool we can drink here!

We went into the first one we spotted.

The Bar Fly

It was deserted.

Except for a wasted man playing himself in pool,

Mmmy shot.

a dog drinking beer out of a tumbler,

and in a corner, four boys.

We immediately paired off.

Hiya!

My boy was already pretty drunk so he went right for it.

Can I kiss you?

I knew this wasn't the kiss I wanted.

No, but you can pick me up.

Uhh, okay.

And there it was.

The magic.

Cute Butt

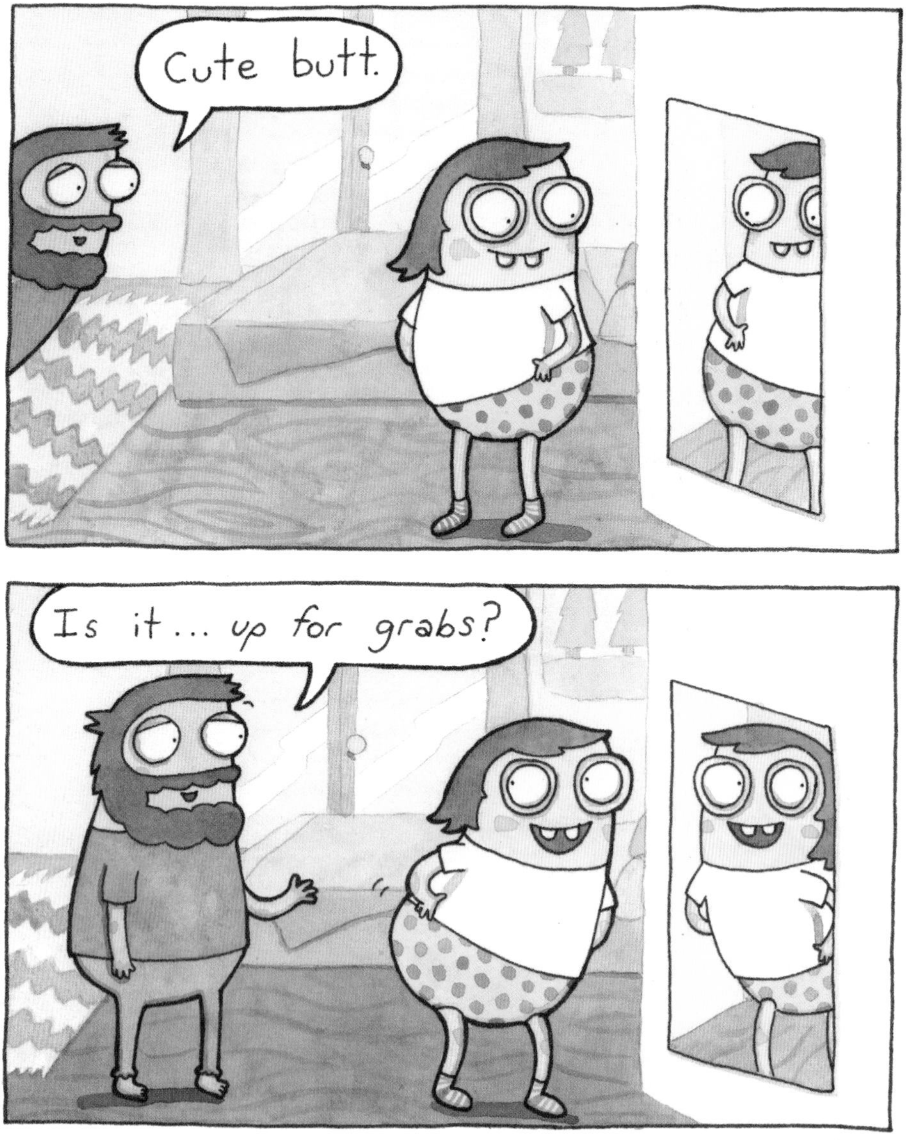
Cute butt.
Is it... up for grabs?

## Twinning

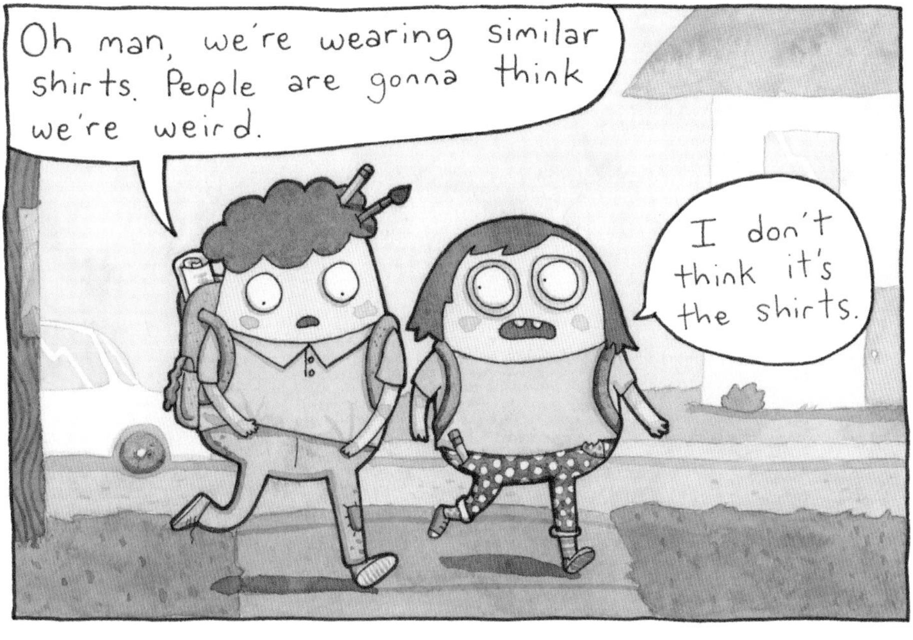
Oh man, we're wearing similar shirts. People are gonna think we're weird.
I don't think it's the shirts.

# Repeat

Whoa, this song is amazing.
Hey, glad ya like me.
REPEAT
REPEAT
REPEAT
REPEAT
REPEAT
REPEAT
REPE
REPE
REPEAT
REPEAT
REPEAT
REPEAT
REPEAT
REPEAT

## Snuggle

What would you do with Butter Udder if I died?
Would you keep her?
Yeah, I'd keep her.
Would you snuggle her?
Yeah.
I'd snuggle her.
Good.

# My First Boyfriend

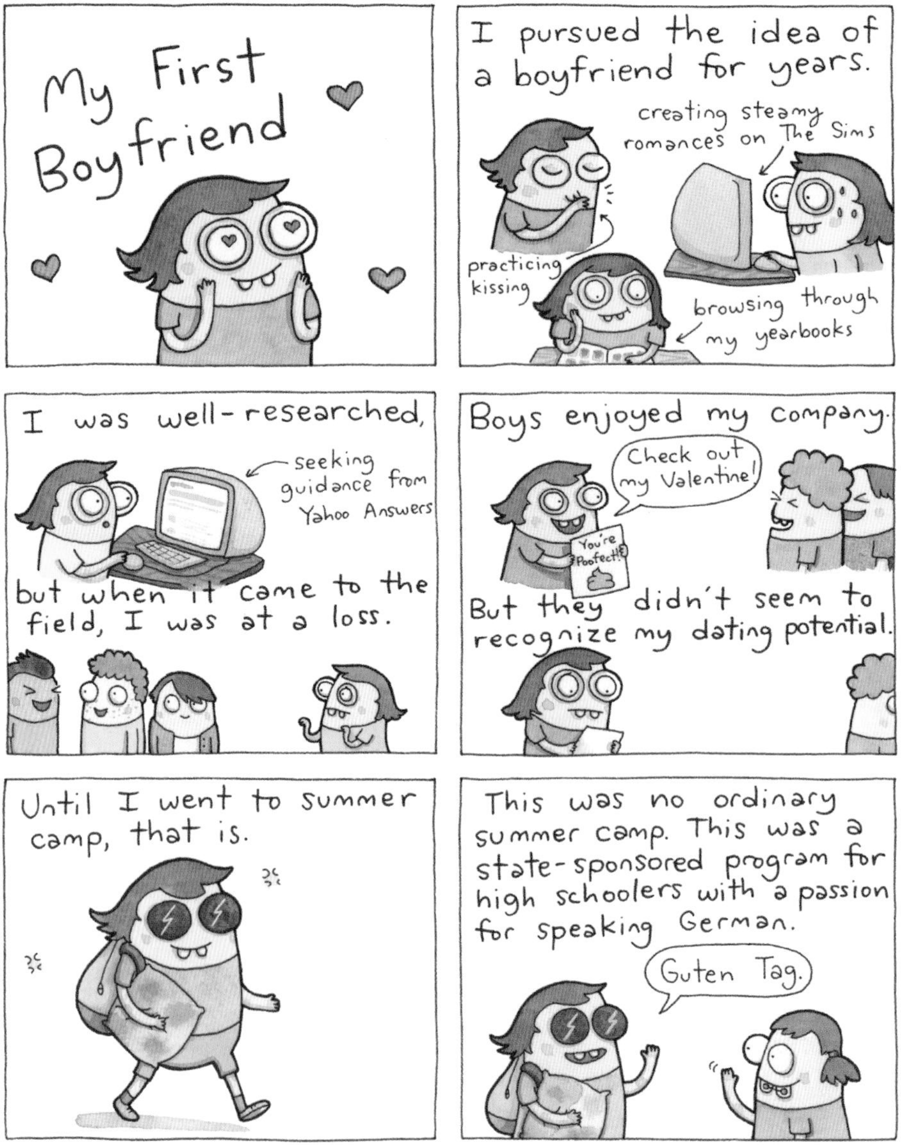
My First Boyfriend
I pursued the idea of a boyfriend for years.
creating steamy romances on The Sims
practicing kissing
browsing through my yearbooks
I was well-researched,
seeking guidance from Yahoo Answers
but when it came to the field, I was at a loss.
Boys enjoyed my company.
Check out my Valentine!
You're Poofect!
But they didn't seem to recognize my dating potential.
Until I went to summer camp, that is.
This was no ordinary summer camp. This was a state-sponsored program for high schoolers with a passion for speaking German.
Guten Tag.

Finally, among my fellow language nerds,

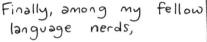

was my chance to prove my date-ability!

I would find a boy and charm him with clever German puns,

You're the wurst!

with my basic knowledge of friendship bracelet patterns,

and with my greatest advantage of all...

process of elimination!

already in a relationship | deathly afraid of spiders and eye contact | a little weird, but <u>Single!!!</u>

Hallo.

My First Boyfriend

Okay, turns out he was more like my first friend that happened to be a boy.

we played lots of games

He tried teaching me how to dance

we had adorable picnics during camp

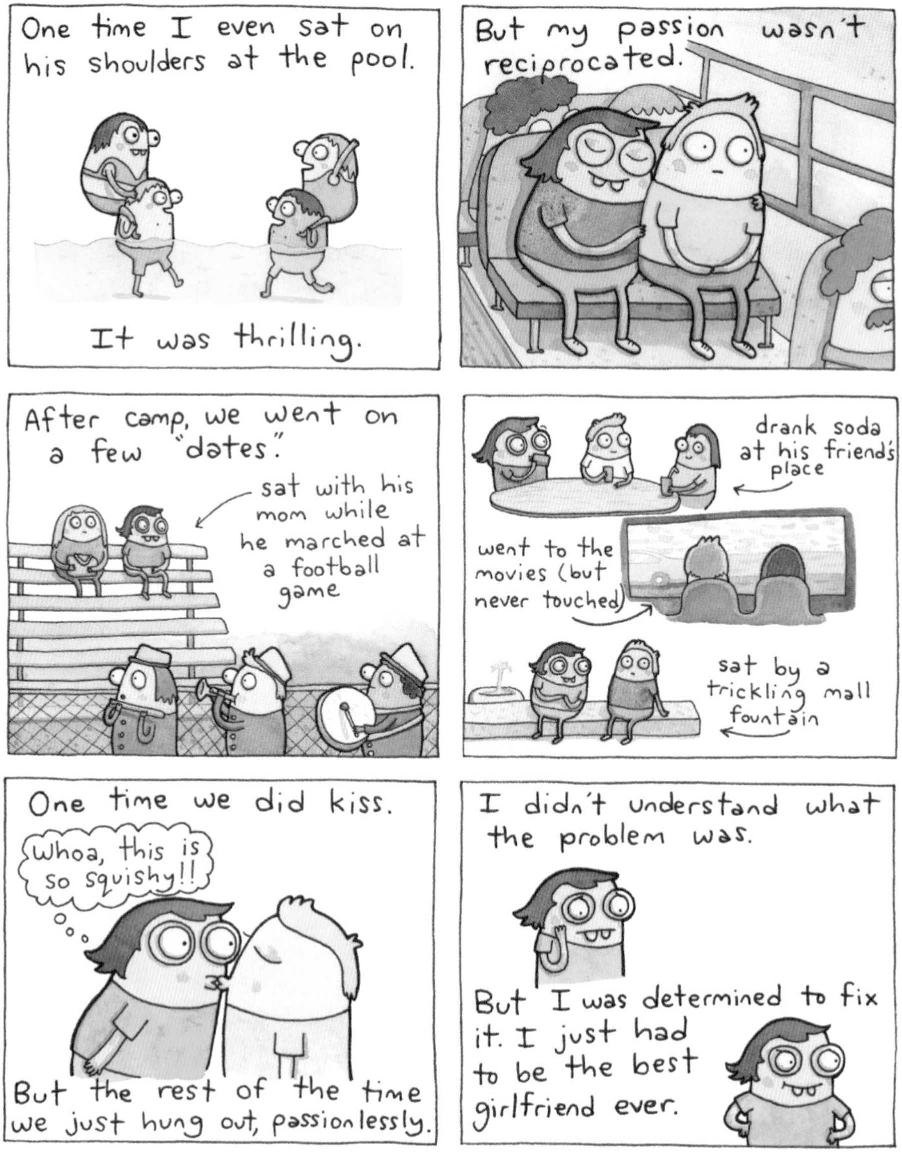
One time I even sat on his shoulders at the pool.
It was thrilling.
But my passion wasn't reciprocated.
After camp, we went on a few "dates."
sat with his mom while he marched at a football game
drank soda at his friend's place
went to the movies (but never touched)
sat by a trickling mall fountain
One time we did kiss.
Whoa, this is so squishy!!
But the rest of the time we just hung out, passionlessly.
I didn't understand what the problem was.
But I was determined to fix it. I just had to be the best girlfriend ever.

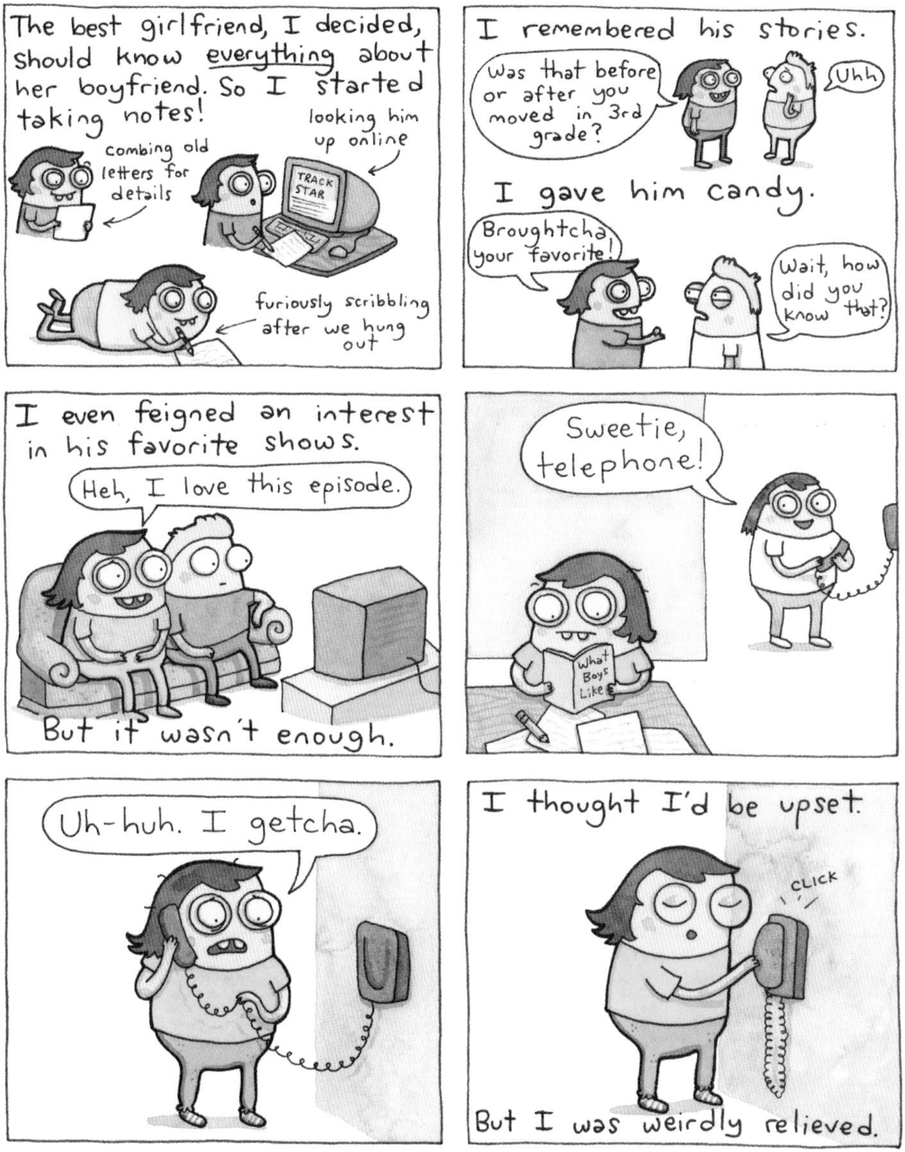
The best girlfriend, I decided, should know everything about her boyfriend. So I started taking notes!
combing old letters for details
looking him up online
TRACK STAR
furiously scribbling after we hung out
I remembered his stories.
Was that before or after you moved in 3rd grade?
Uhh
I gave him candy.
Broughtcha your favorite!
Wait, how did you know that?
I even feigned an interest in his favorite shows.
Heh, I love this episode.
But it wasn't enough.
Sweetie, telephone!
What Boys Like
Uh-huh. I getcha.
I thought I'd be upset.
CLICK
But I was weirdly relieved.

Once we broke up, it was like I could finally go back to being myself.

And I could say...

I'd had a boyfriend in high school!

Yes!

How to Get Rich Makin' Art
Please tell me if you know.

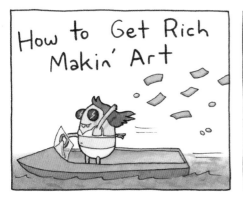

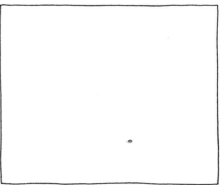

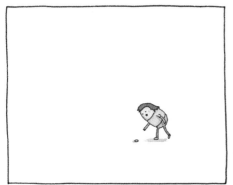

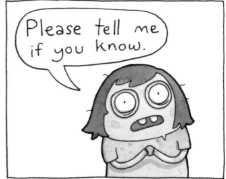

One of my closest friends growing up was my cow plushie Butter Udder.

We did everything together.

I'd often make her speak for me.

I love this show!

Butter Udder was one of the earliest ways I remember advocating for myself.

Please tuck me in.

She said things I wasn't brave enough to say.

I don't want to play anymore.

She demanded things I wasn't strong enough to demand for myself.

Leave me alone!

When I was Butter Udder, it felt safe to explore my identity, to push boundaries.

Wanna hear my new song?

Fine.

If someone didn't like what she said, they weren't rejecting me, only her.

That was terrible.

Oopsie doodle!

I can't carry Butter Udder around anymore.
*inhale
I'm too old for that.
So I use comics.

## Self-Destruct

Um, Captain?
Why are these buttons so close together?
self-explore
self-destruct

The other day...

I found a potato in a parking lot.

Yesss, I get to sleep in my favorite shirt again tonight!
0:30
With my favorite plushies.
Do you enjoy your world of cozy illusions?

## Alone Time

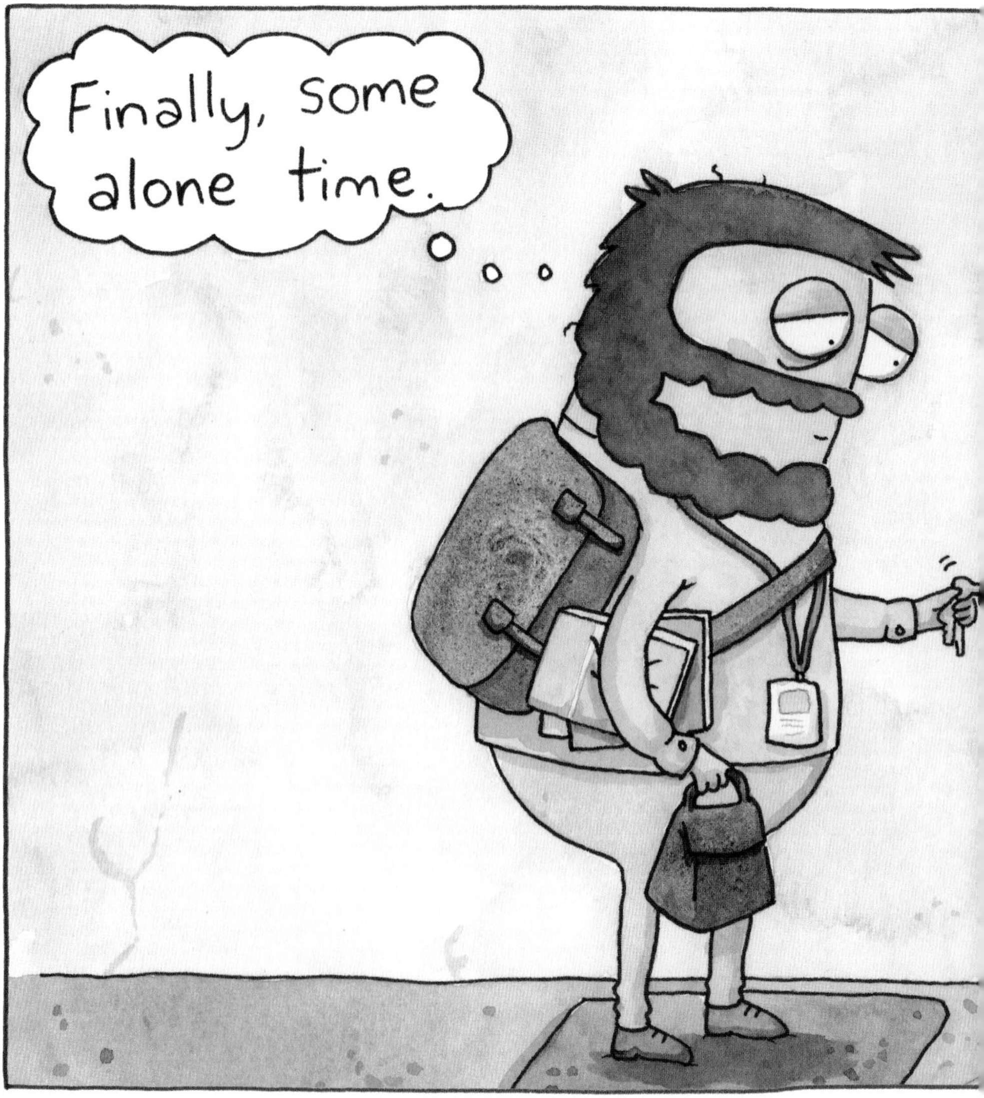
Finally, some alone time.

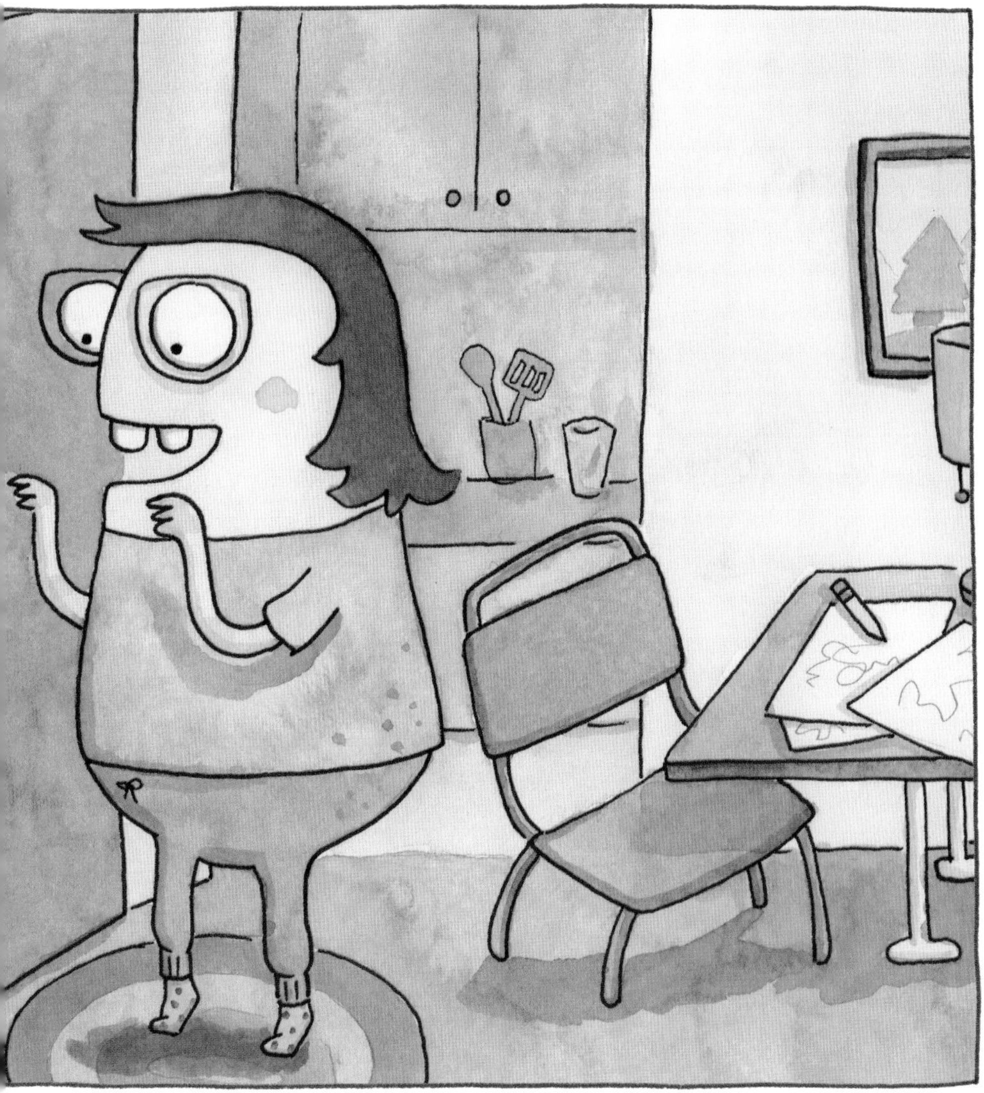

# Five Minutes

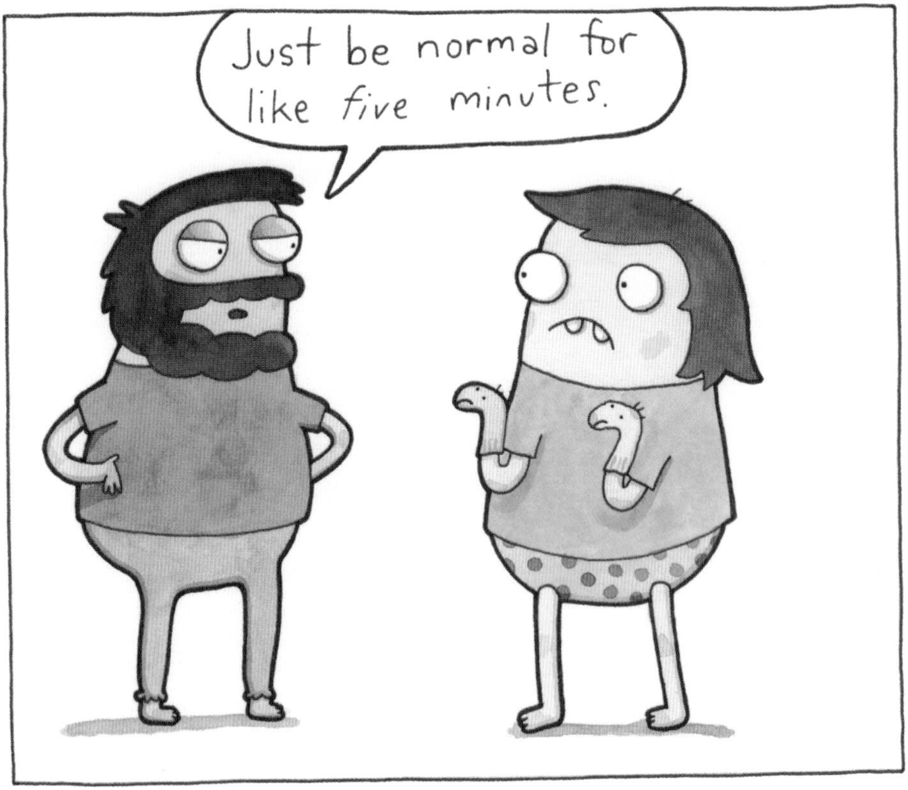
Just be normal for like *five* minutes.

# Like Who I Am

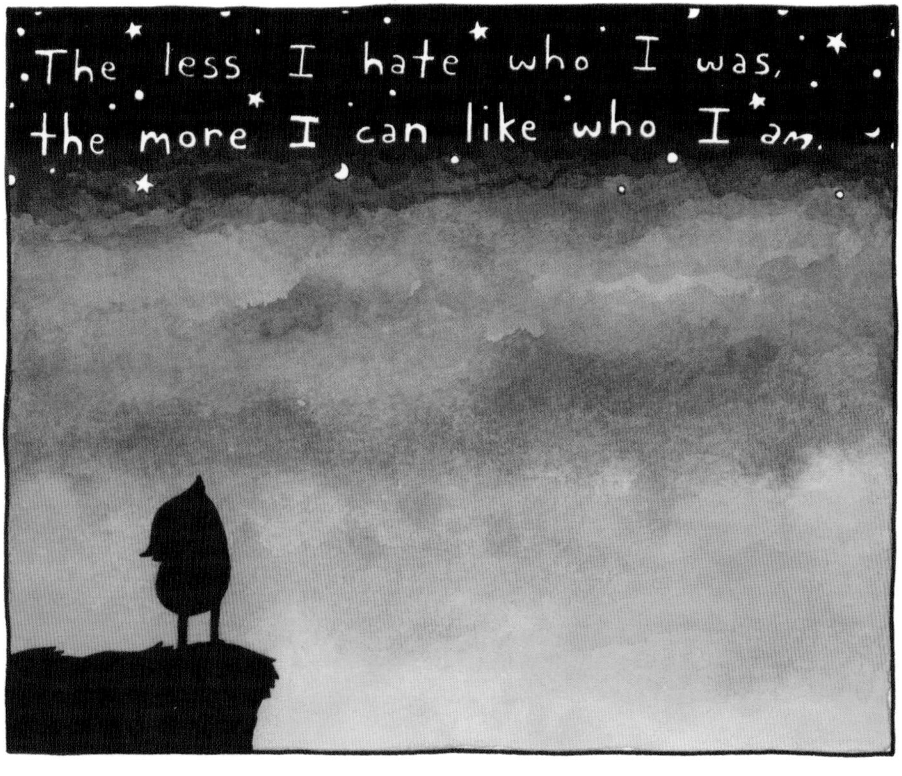
The less I hate who I was,
the more I can like who I am.

## Estimation

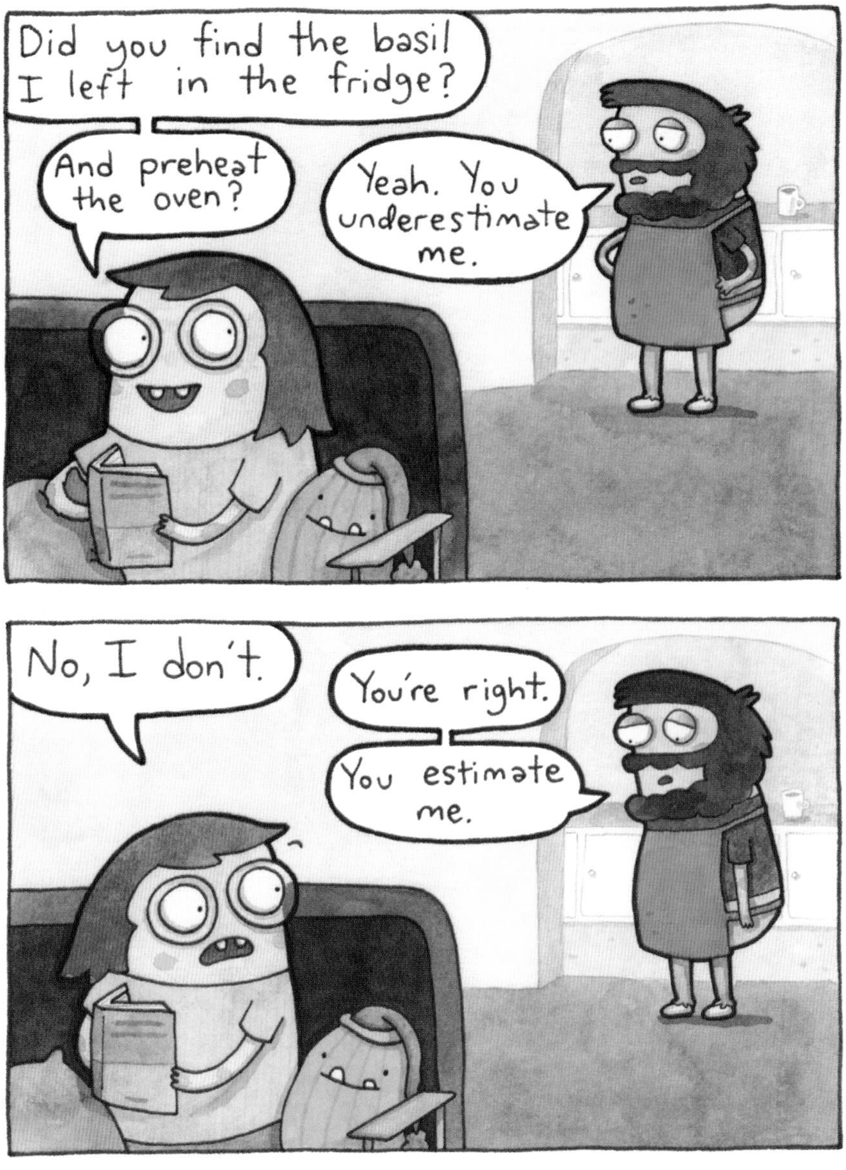
Did you find the basil I left in the fridge?
And preheat the oven?
Yeah. You underestimate me.
No, I don't.
You're right.
You estimate me.

Asking for help doesn't mean you're weak.

It means you're strong enough to know your limits.

-POP-

Besides, victories are better when they're shared.

CRUNCH CRUNCH

No matter how small.

PICKLES

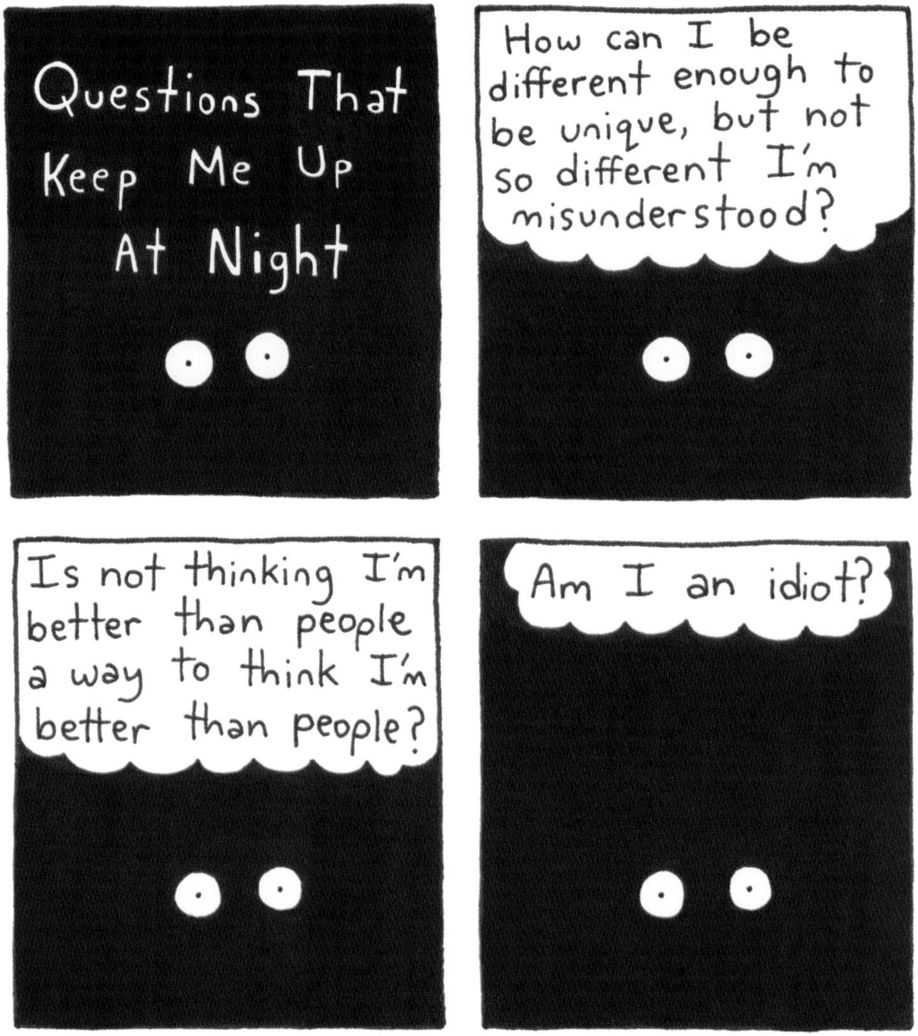
Questions That Keep Me Up At Night
How can I be different enough to be unique, but not so different I'm misunderstood?
Is not thinking I'm better than people a way to think I'm better than people?
Am I an idiot?

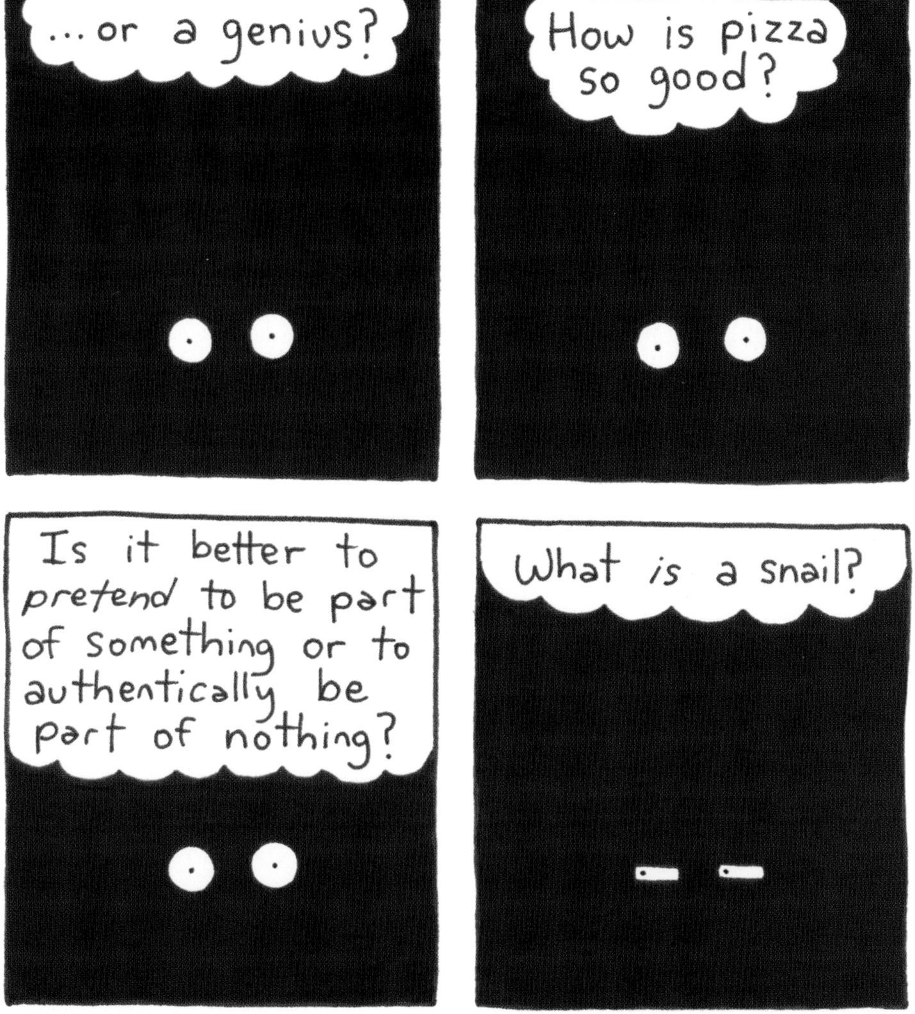
...or a genius?
How is pizza so good?
Is it better to *pretend* to be part of something or to authentically be part of nothing?
What *is* a snail?

# My Landlord

My landlord is overworked.
Uh-huh. And you're where?
CLOGS BE GONE
Whenever I see him, he's doing like 4 things.
One time he came to my apartment to fix my leaky ceiling.
Let's see what we got here.
To find the leak, he decided he had to saw into the ceiling.
Well, here goes nothin'.
So I watched him from my couch.
Say, dontcha want safety goggles?
No time.
BZZZZZ
BRING BRING
Right before he sawed into the ceiling, his phone rang.
Yeah, what's up?
BZZZZZ
And he answered it!
AHHH MY EYES!!

## How Annoying

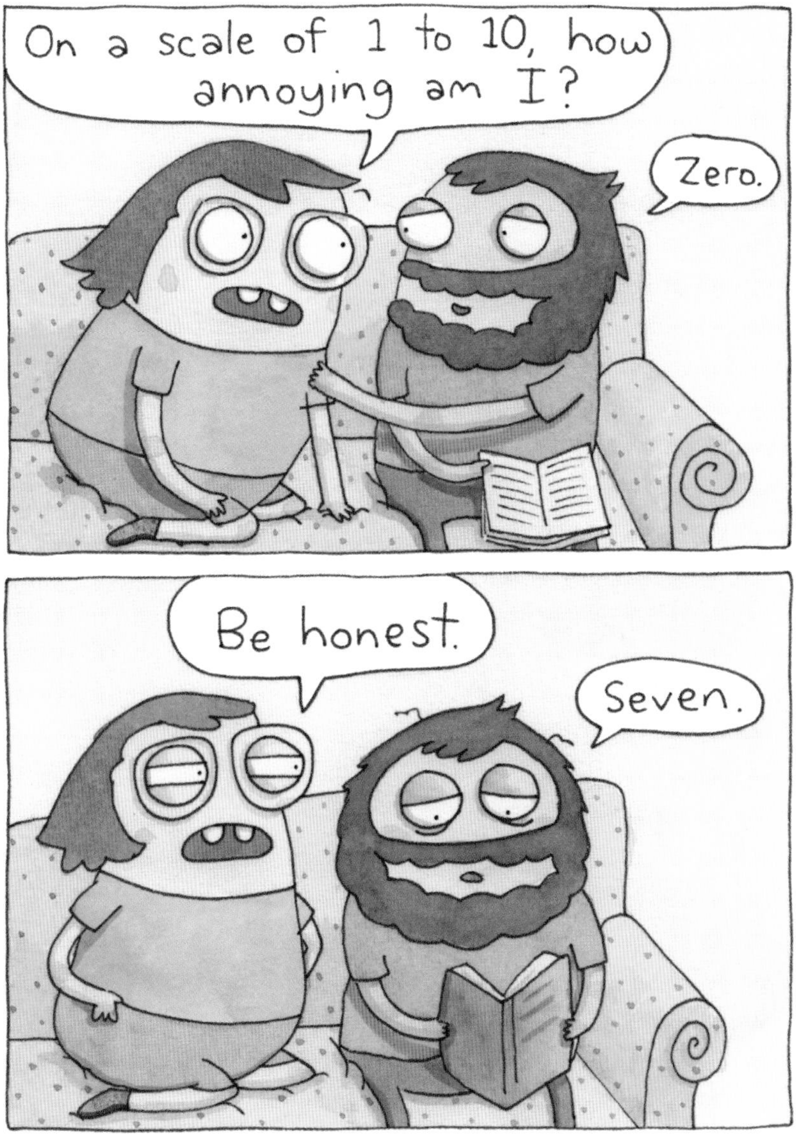
On a scale of 1 to 10, how annoying am I?
Zero.
Be honest.
Seven.

# 20 Amazing Feelings

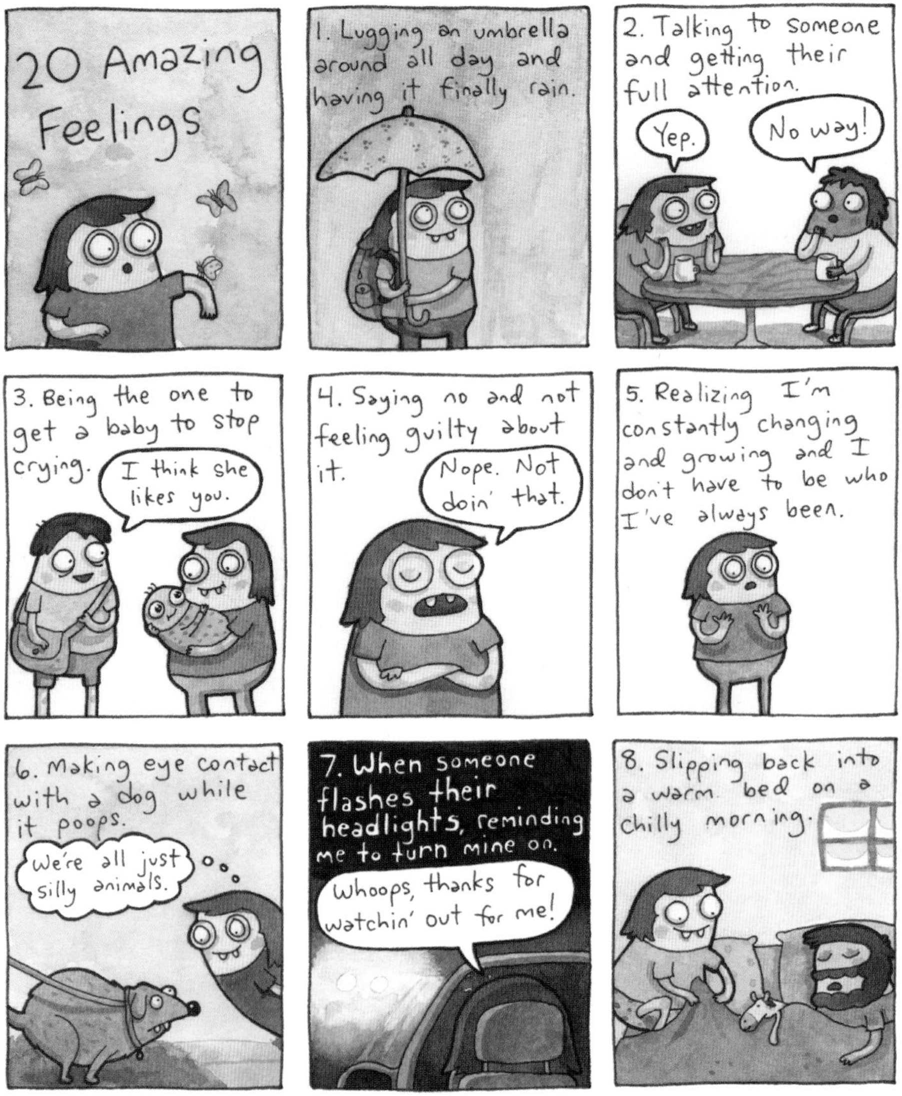
20 Amazing Feelings
1. Lugging an umbrella around all day and having it finally rain.
2. Talking to someone and getting their full attention.
Yep.
No way!
3. Being the one to get a baby to stop crying.
I think she likes you.
4. Saying no and not feeling guilty about it.
Nope. Not doin' that.
5. Realizing I'm constantly changing and growing and I don't have to be who I've always been.
6. Making eye contact with a dog while it poops.
We're all just silly animals.
7. When someone flashes their headlights, reminding me to turn mine on.
Whoops, thanks for watchin' out for me!
8. Slipping back into a warm bed on a chilly morning.

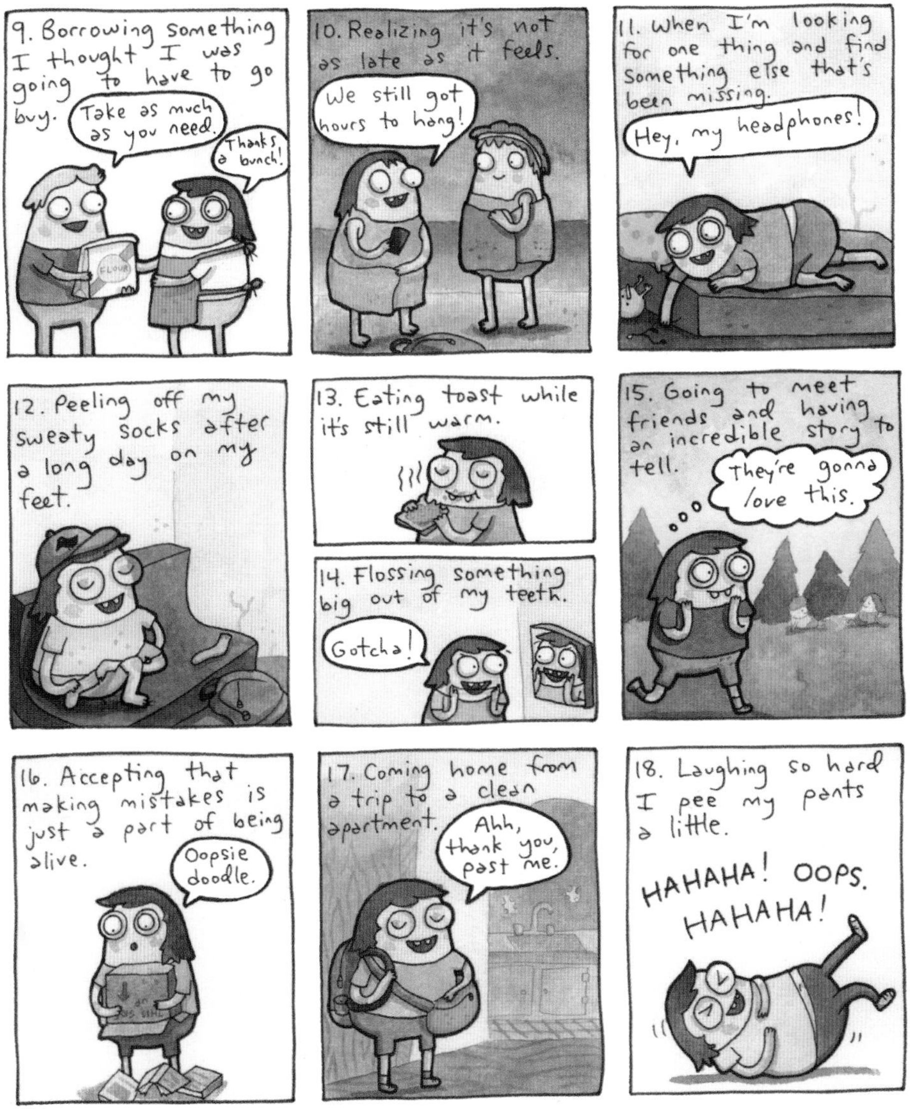
9. Borrowing something I thought I was going to have to go buy.
Take as much as you need.
Thanks a bunch!
FLOUR
10. Realizing it's not as late as it feels.
We still got hours to hang!
11. When I'm looking for one thing and find something else that's been missing.
Hey, my headphones!
12. Peeling off my sweaty socks after a long day on my feet.
13. Eating toast while it's still warm.
14. Flossing something big out of my teeth.
Gotcha!
15. Going to meet friends and having an incredible story to tell.
They're gonna love this.
16. Accepting that making mistakes is just a part of being alive.
Oopsie doodle.
17. Coming home from a trip to a clean apartment.
Ahh, thank you, past me.
18. Laughing so hard I pee my pants a little.
HAHAHA! OOPS. HAHAHA!

19. When something good happens to a character I love.

20. Not really knowing where I am, but having nowhere to be.

## Get Your Bag

Hey -
I was thinking I might leave for a few days.
Go camping. See my dad.
Really?!
When ya going?
That's great!
Lemme get your bag!
Oh.

# Two People

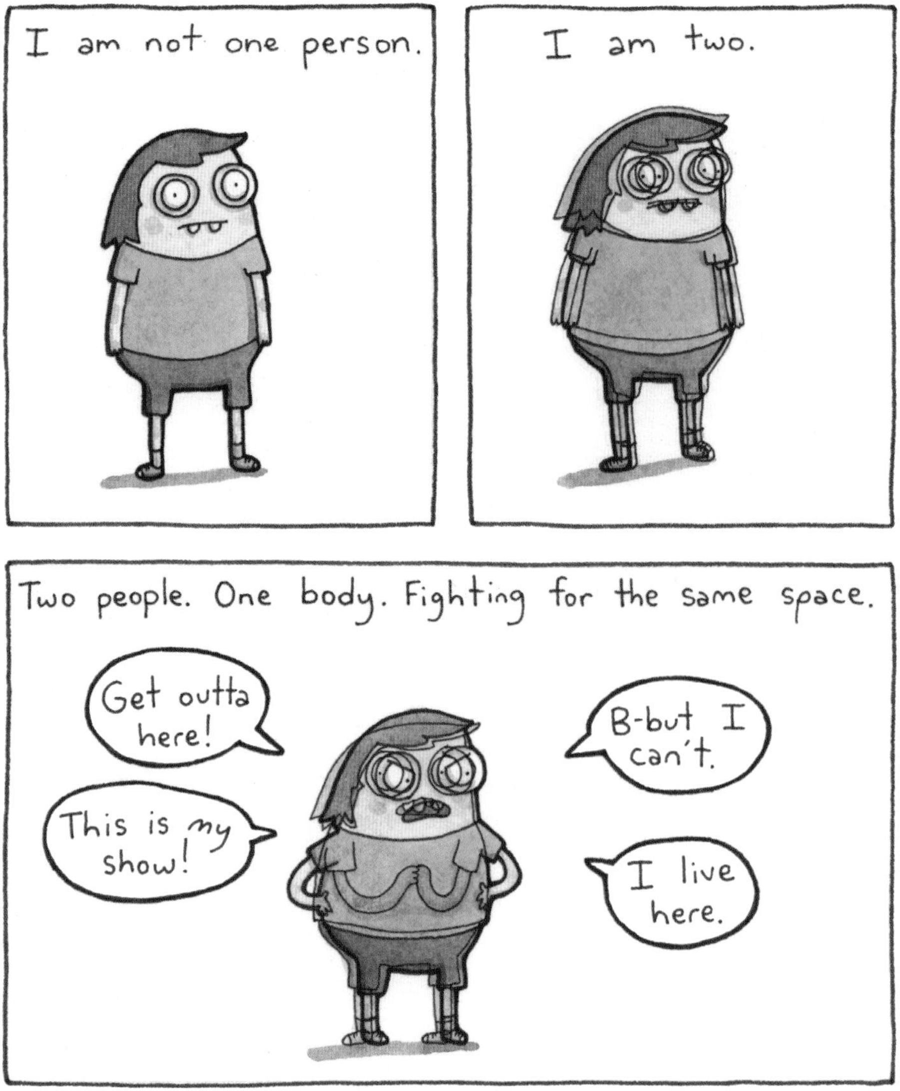
I am not one person.
I am two.
Two people. One body. Fighting for the same space.
Get outta here!
B-but I can't.
This is my show!
I live here.

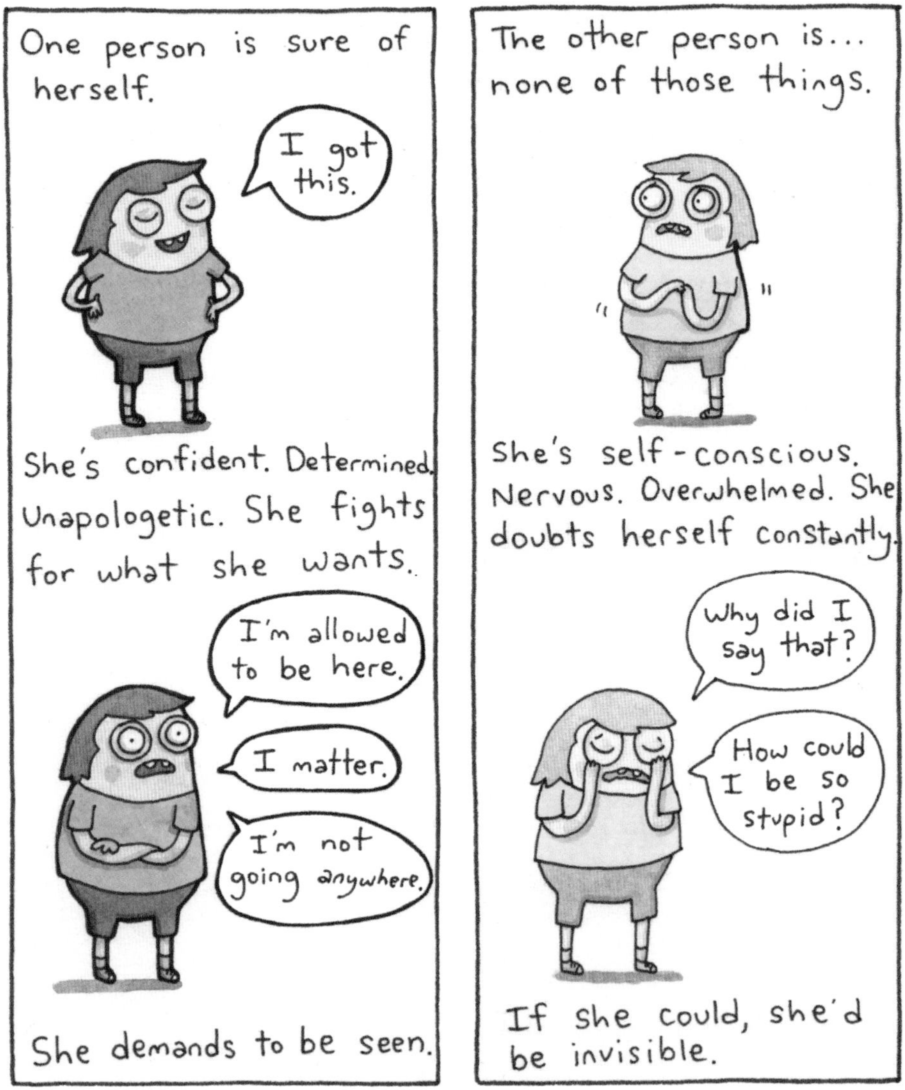
One person is sure of herself.
I got this.
She's confident. Determined. Unapologetic. She fights for what she wants.
I'm allowed to be here.
I matter.
I'm not going anywhere.
She demands to be seen.
The other person is... none of those things.
She's self-conscious. Nervous. Overwhelmed. She doubts herself constantly.
Why did I say that?
How could I be so stupid?
If she could, she'd be invisible.

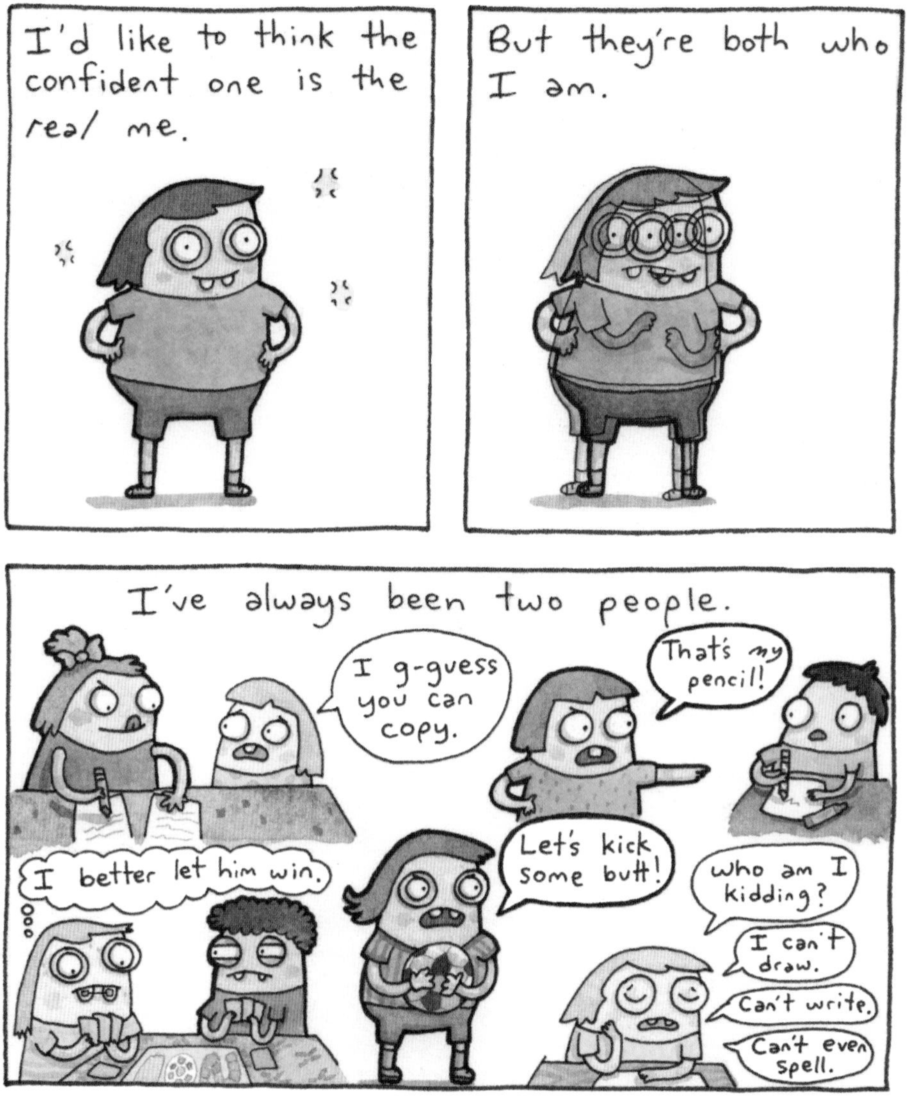
I'd like to think the confident one is the real me.
But they're both who I am.
I've always been two people.
I g-guess you can copy.
That's my pencil!
I better let him win.
Let's kick some butt!
Who am I kidding?
I can't draw.
Can't write.
Can't even spell.

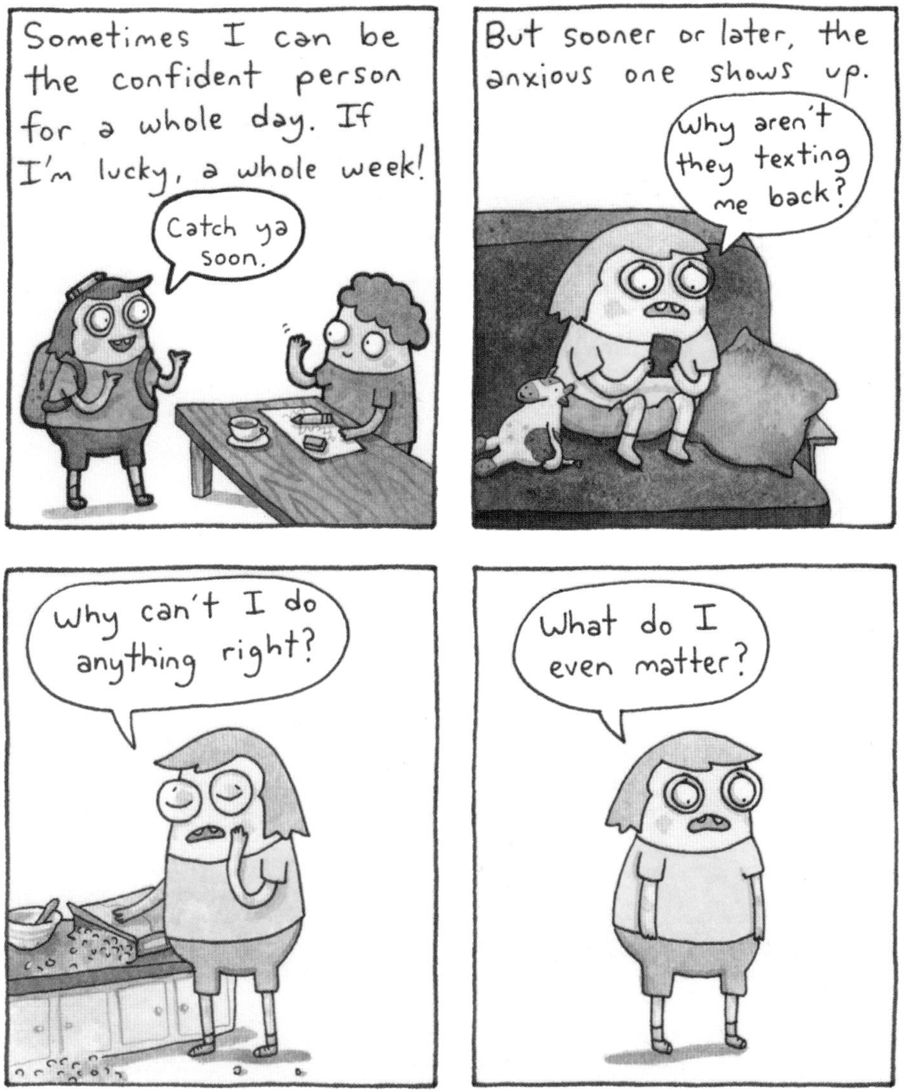
Sometimes I can be the confident person for a whole day. If I'm lucky, a whole week!
Catch ya soon.
But sooner or later, the anxious one shows up.
Why aren't they texting me back?
Why can't I do anything right?
What do I even matter?

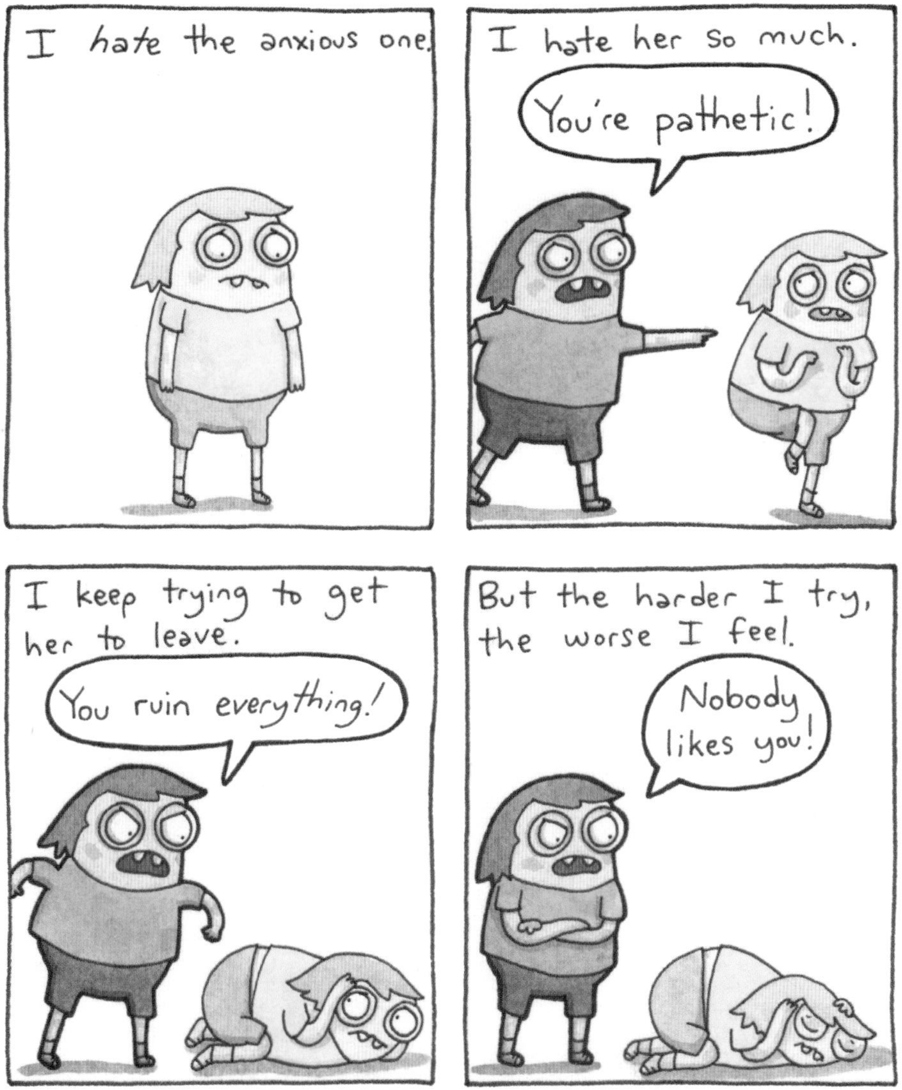
I hate the anxious one.
I hate her so much.
You're pathetic!
I keep trying to get her to leave.
You ruin everything!
But the harder I try, the worse I feel.
Nobody likes you!

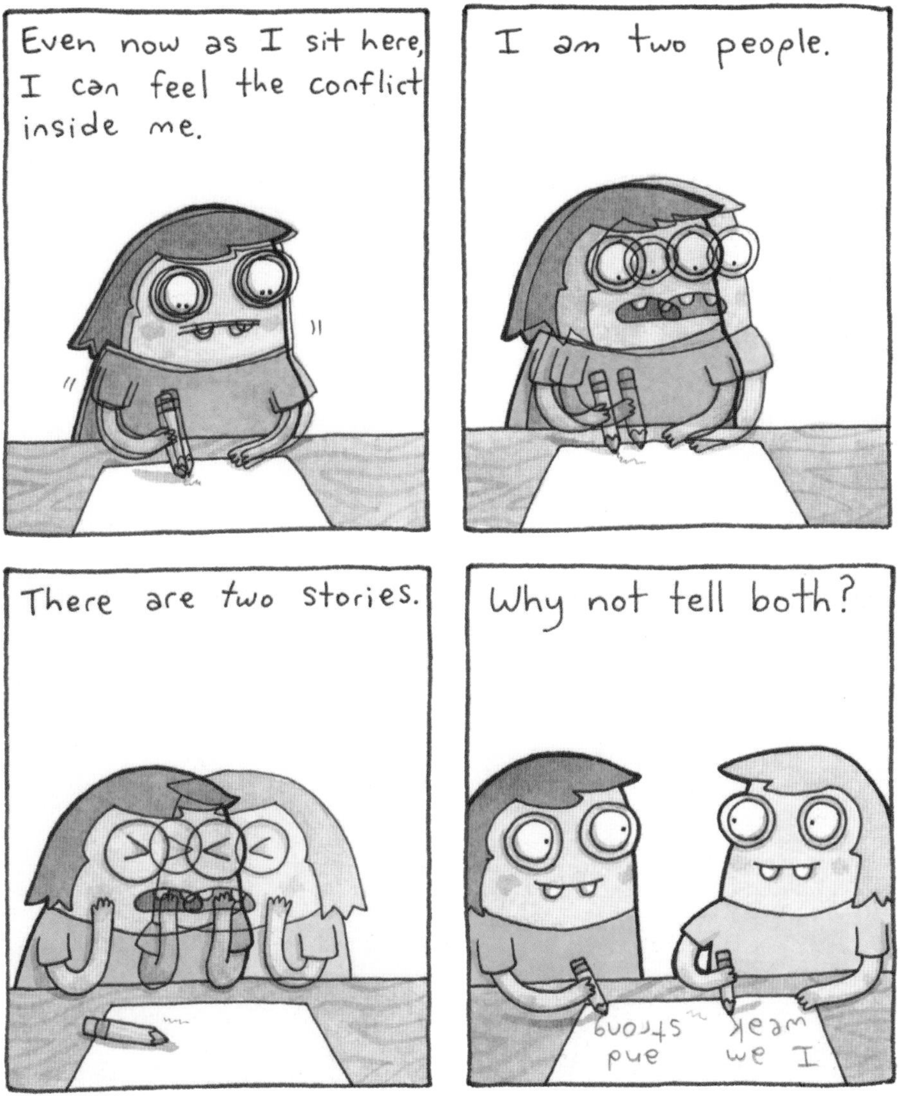
Even now as I sit here, I can feel the conflict inside me.
I am two people.
There are two stories.
Why not tell both?
I am weak and strong

Can't Hug

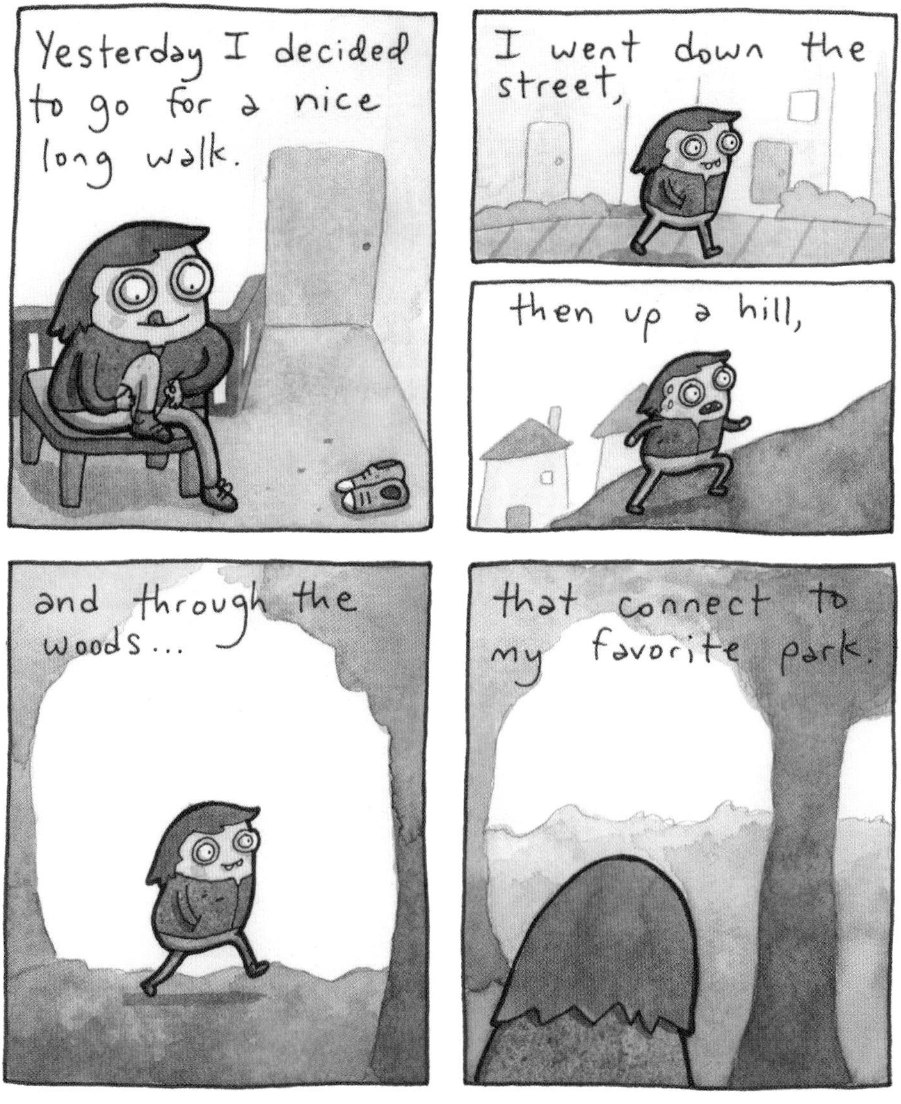
Yesterday I decided to go for a nice long walk.
I went down the street,
then up a hill,
and through the woods...
that connect to my favorite park.

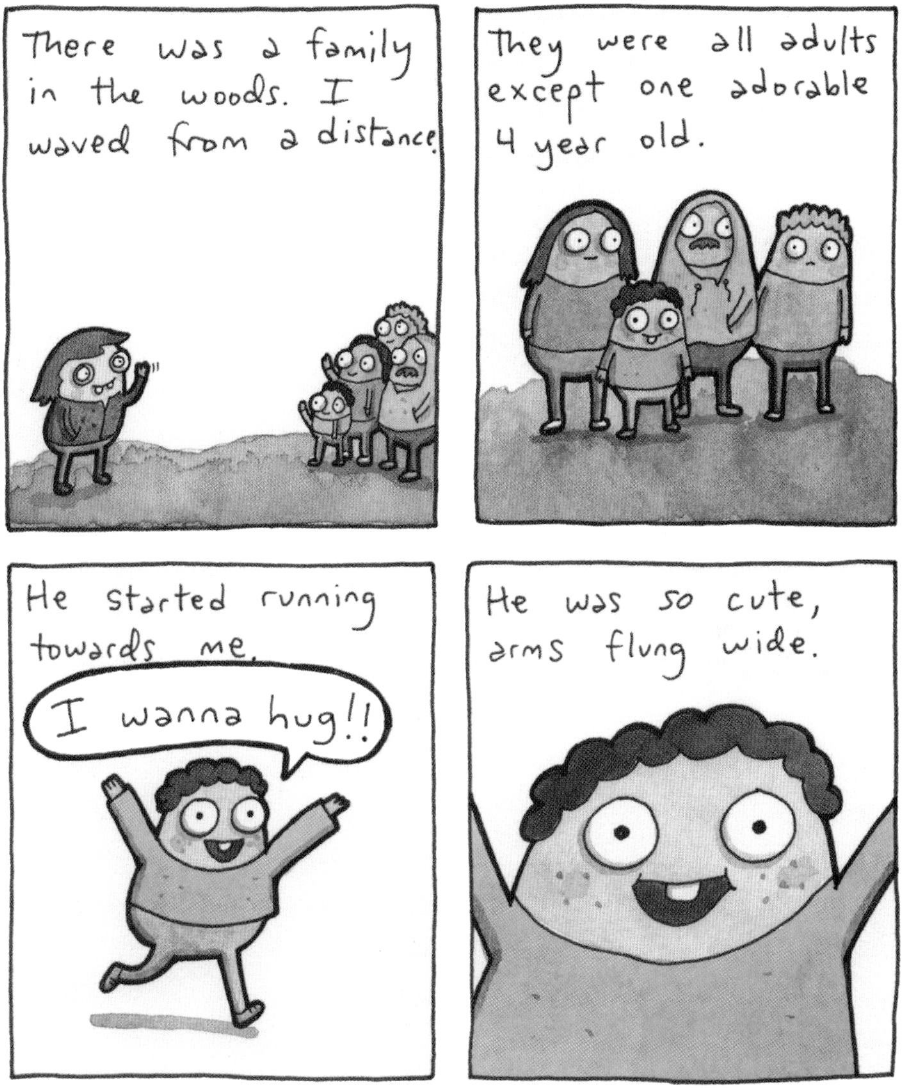
There was a family in the woods. I waved from a distance.
They were all adults except one adorable 4 year old.
He started running towards me.
I wanna hug!!
He was so cute, arms flung wide.

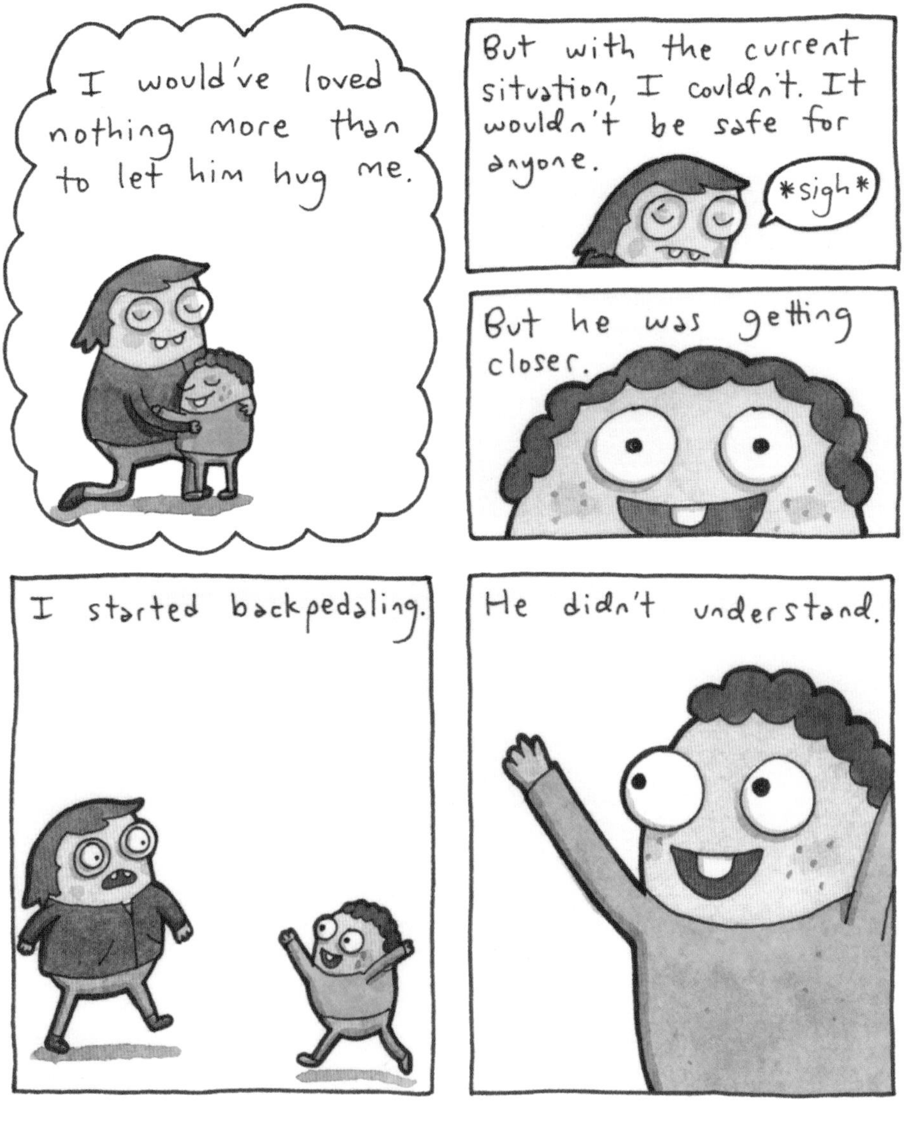
I would've loved nothing more than to let him hug me.
But with the current situation, I couldn't. It wouldn't be safe for anyone.
*sigh*
But he was getting closer.
I started backpedaling.
He didn't understand.

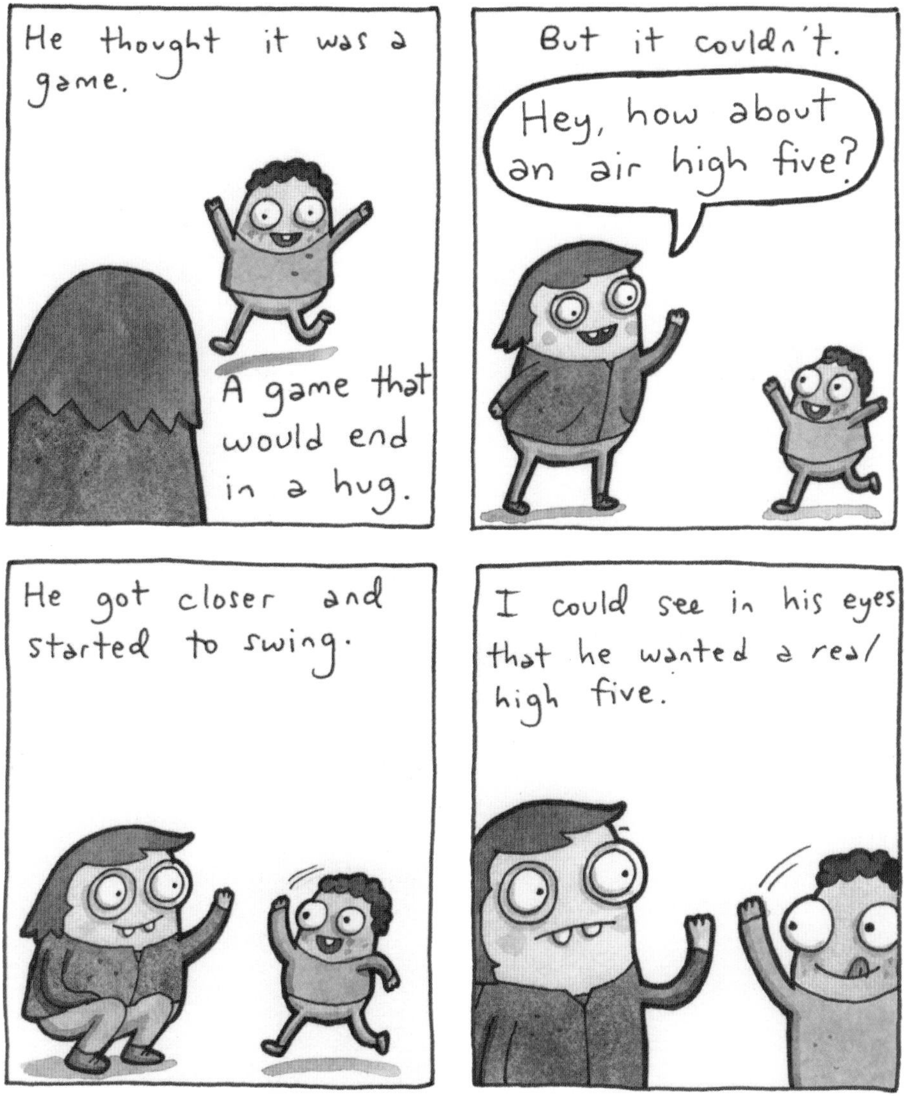
He thought it was a game.
A game that would end in a hug.
But it couldn't.
Hey, how about an air high five?
He got closer and started to swing.
I could see in his eyes that he wanted a real high five.

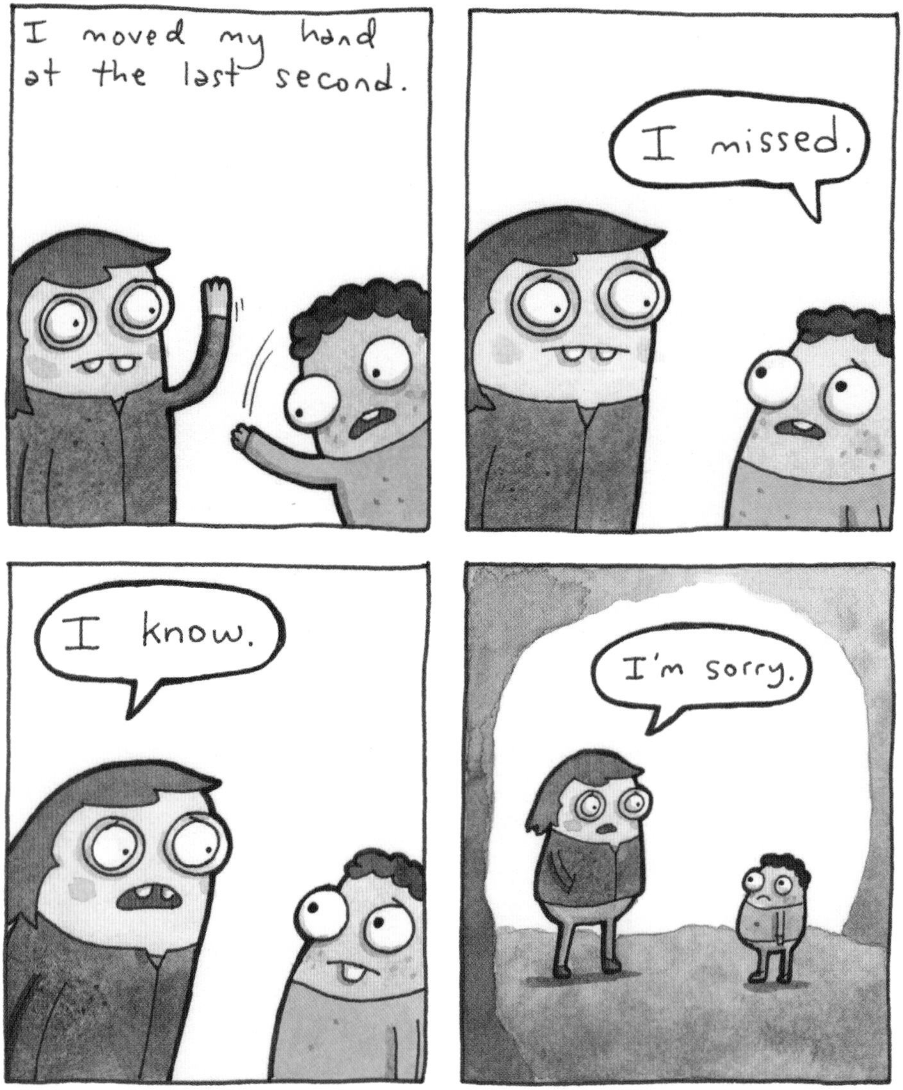

I moved my hand at the last second.
I missed.
I know.
I'm sorry.

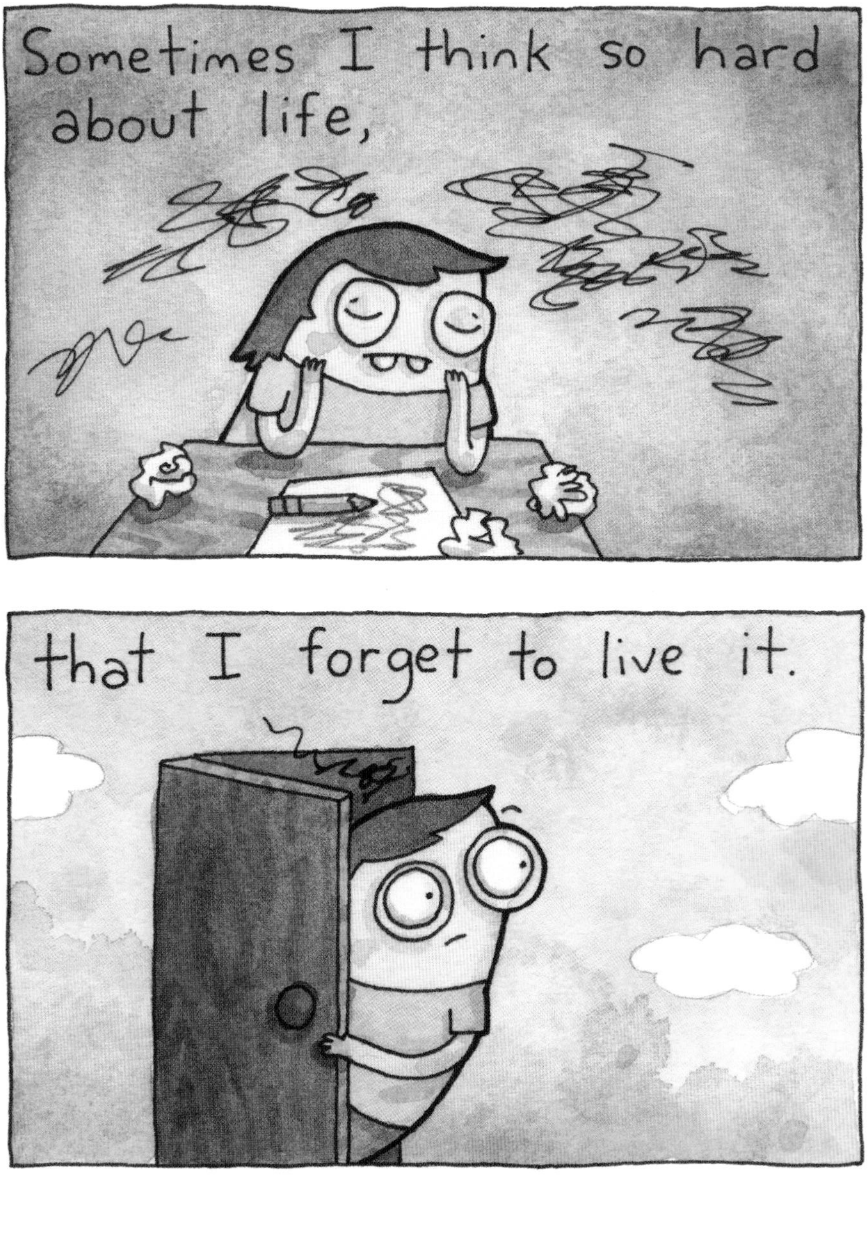
Sometimes I think so hard about life,
that I forget to live it.

Driving home today...

I spotted a Corvette with the license plate:

Y2K

Suddenly something clicked in my head.

"Y" means... "year" and "2K" means...

The Year 2000.

Oh my god.

All this time I thought Y2K was the name of some bug that was gonna eat computers or something.
Y2K
I can't believe it took me this long to figure out.
I...
I'm smartening!

# Butt Cracks

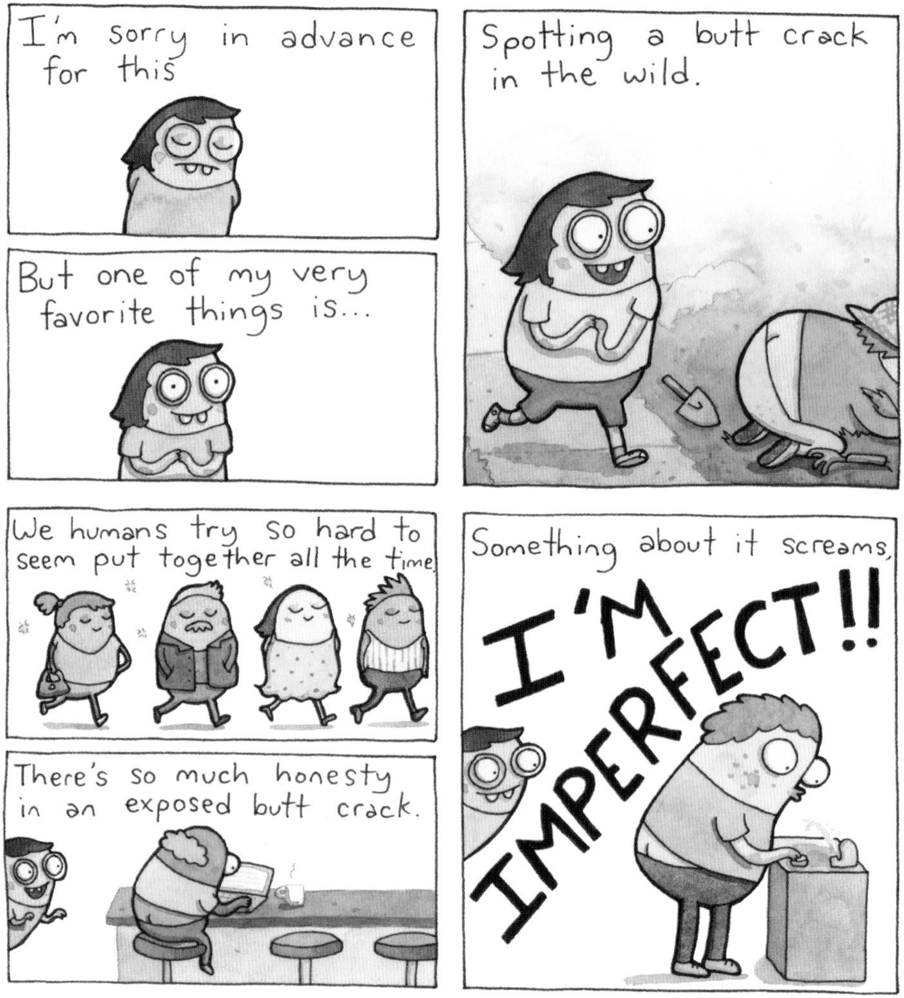
I'm sorry in advance for this
But one of my very favorite things is...
Spotting a butt crack in the wild.
We humans try so hard to seem put together all the time.
There's so much honesty in an exposed butt crack.
Something about it screams,
I'M IMPERFECT!!

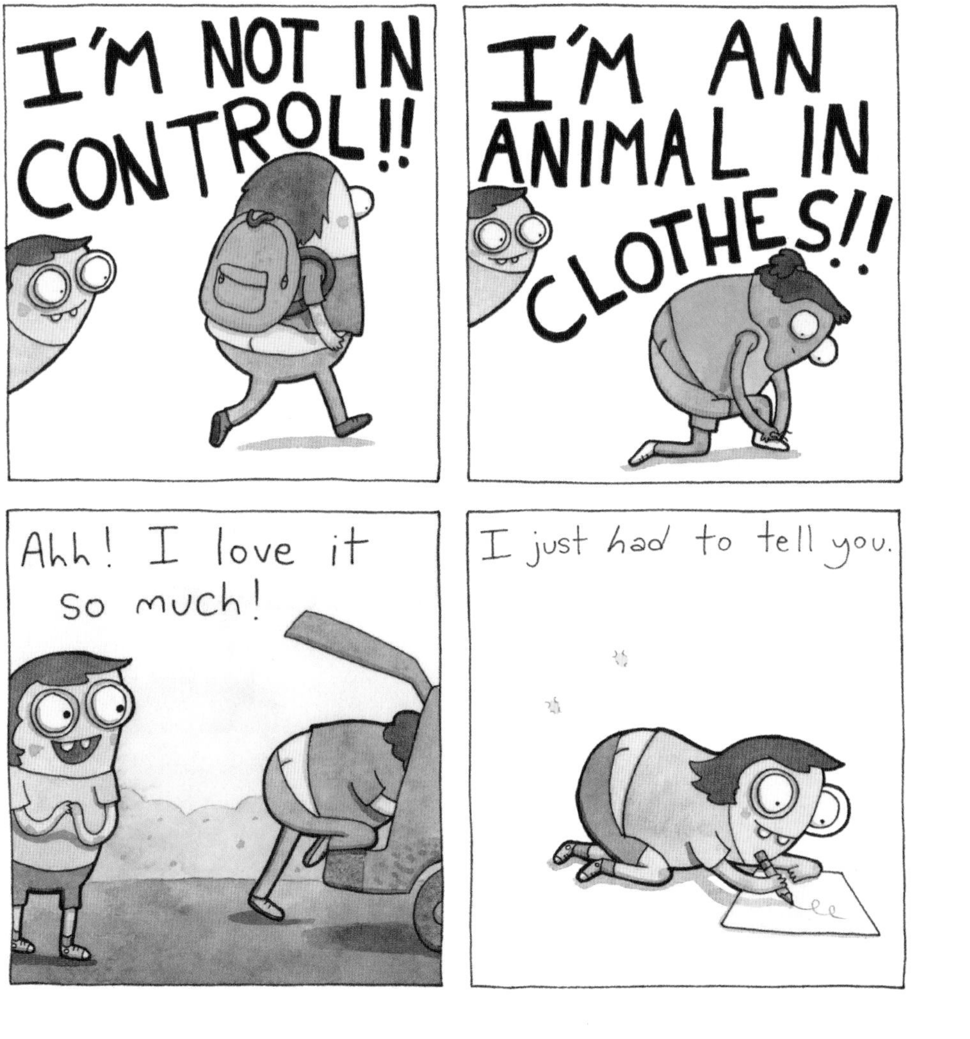
I'M NOT IN CONTROL!!
I'M AN ANIMAL IN CLOTHES!!
Ahh! I love it so much!
I just had to tell you.

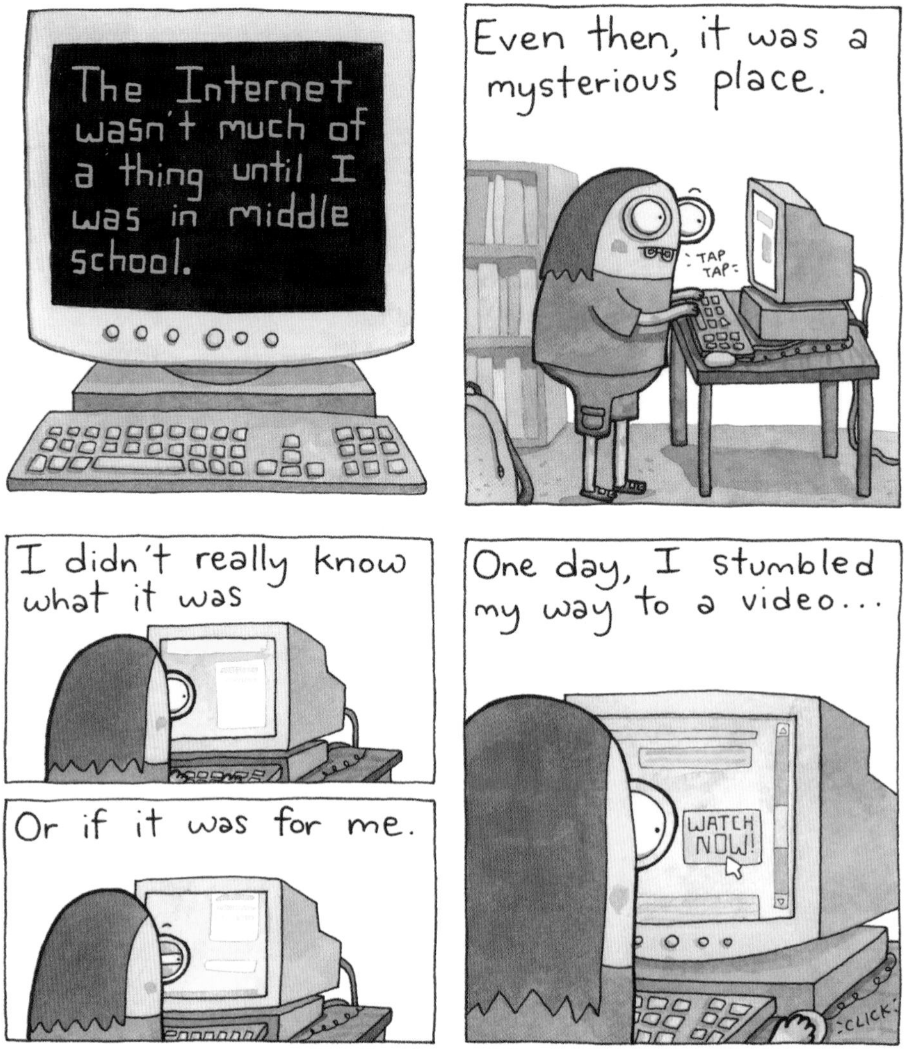
The Internet wasn't much of a thing until I was in middle school.
Even then, it was a mysterious place.
TAP TAP
I didn't really know what it was
Or if it was for me.
One day, I stumbled my way to a video...
WATCH NOW!
CLICK

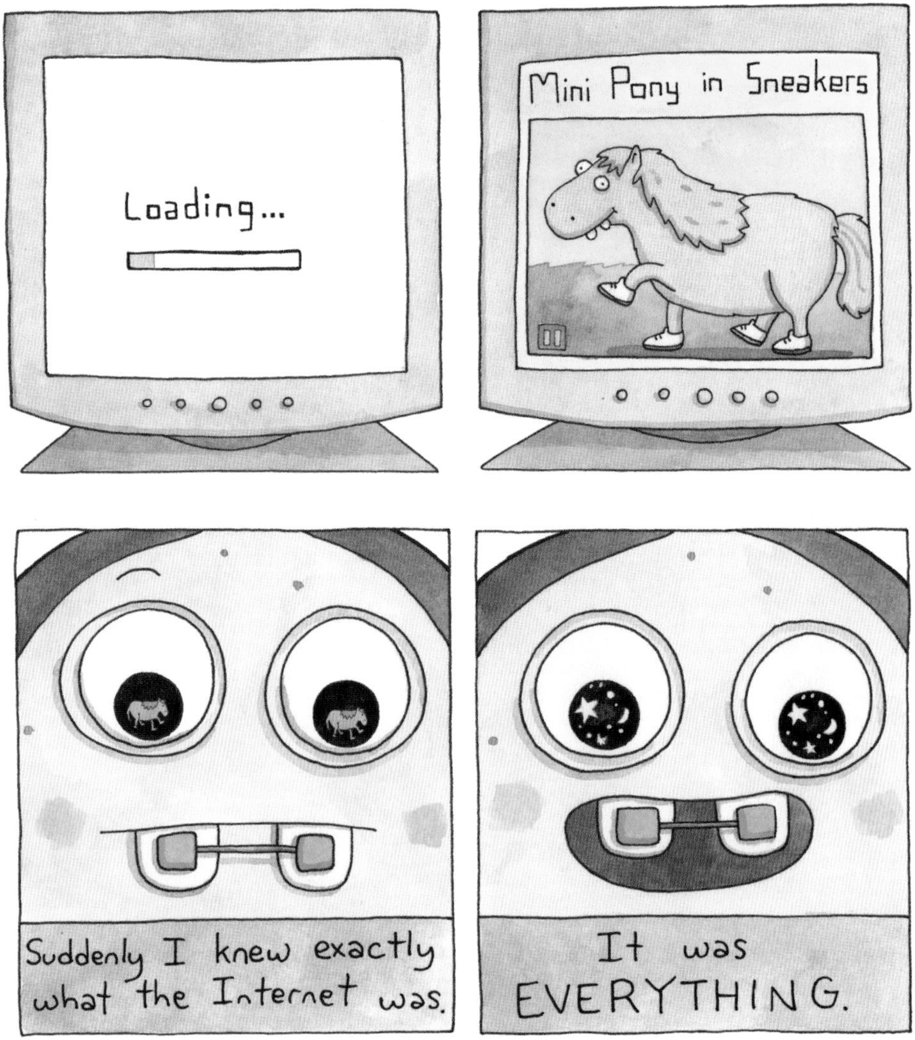
Loading...
Mini Pony in Sneakers
Suddenly I knew exactly what the Internet was.
It was EVERYTHING.

## Rockstar

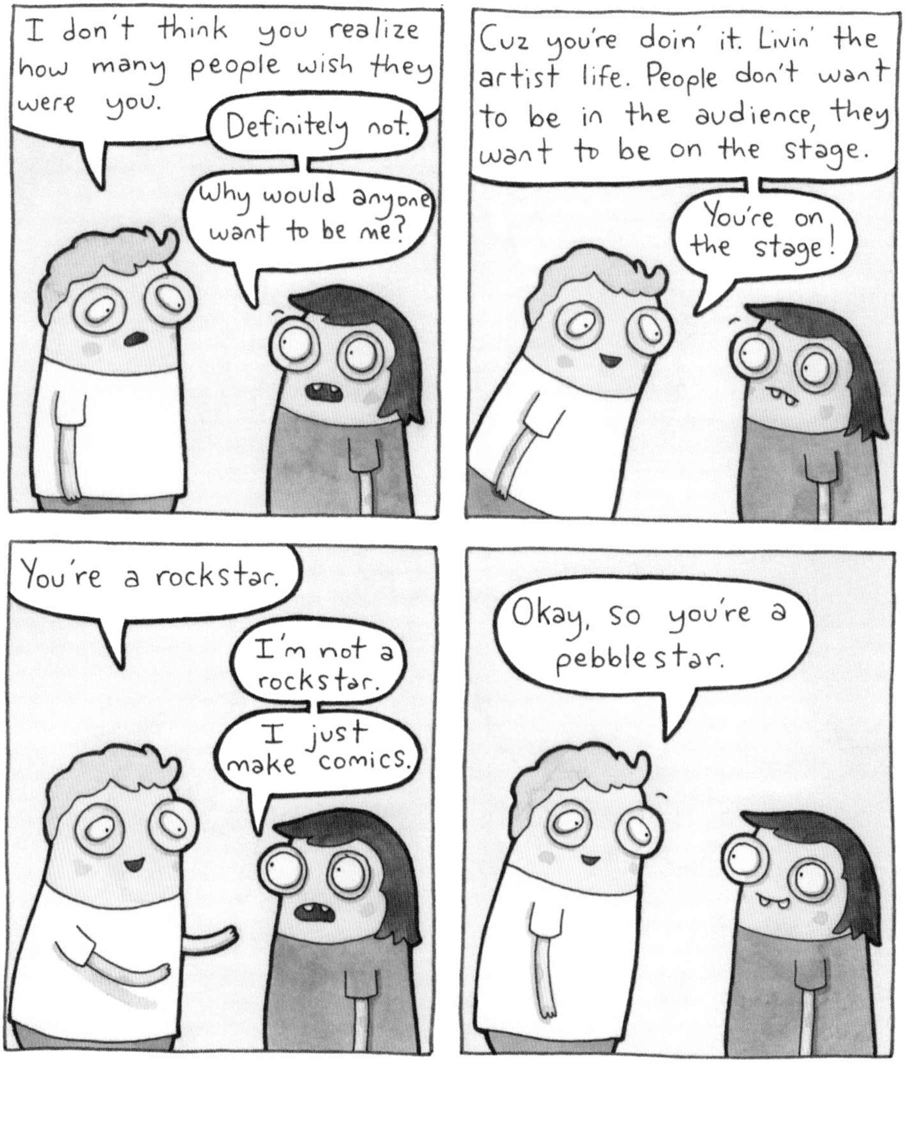
I don't think you realize how many people wish they were you.
Definitely not.
Why would anyone want to be me?
Cuz you're doin' it. Livin' the artist life. People don't want to be in the audience, they want to be on the stage.
You're on the stage!
You're a rockstar.
I'm not a rockstar.
I just make comics.
Okay, so you're a pebblestar.

# Your Favorite Thing

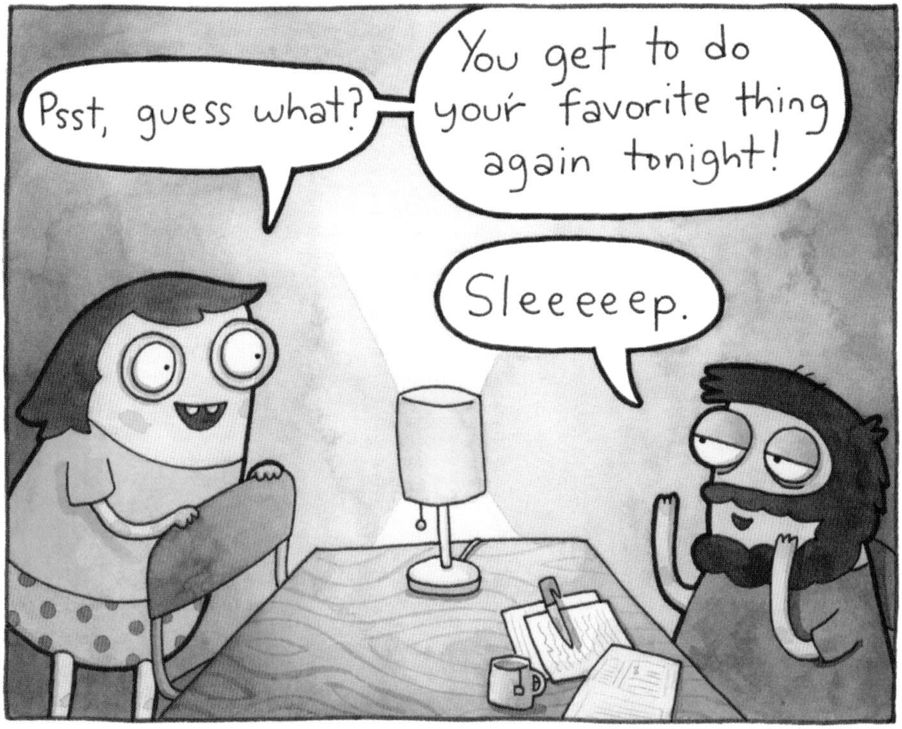
Psst, guess what?
You get to do your favorite thing again tonight!
Sleeeeeep.

## The Best

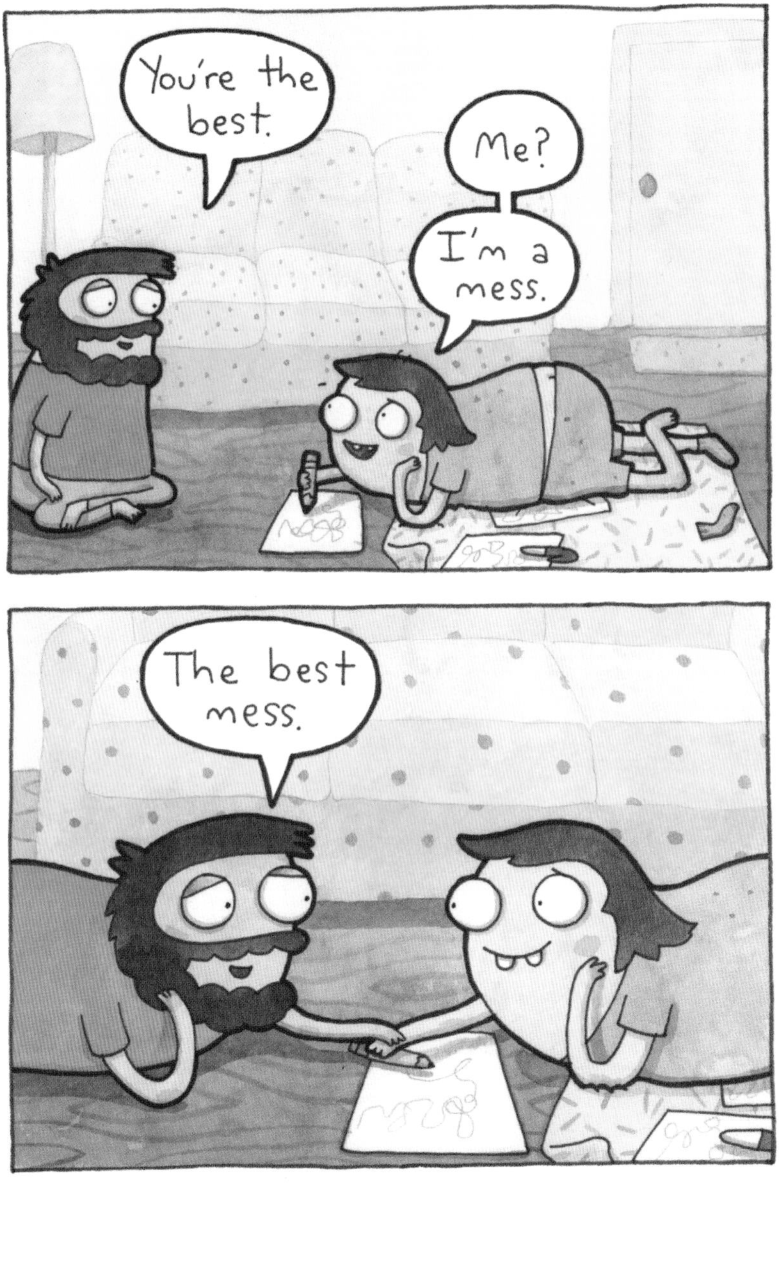
You're the best.
Me?
I'm a mess.
The best mess.

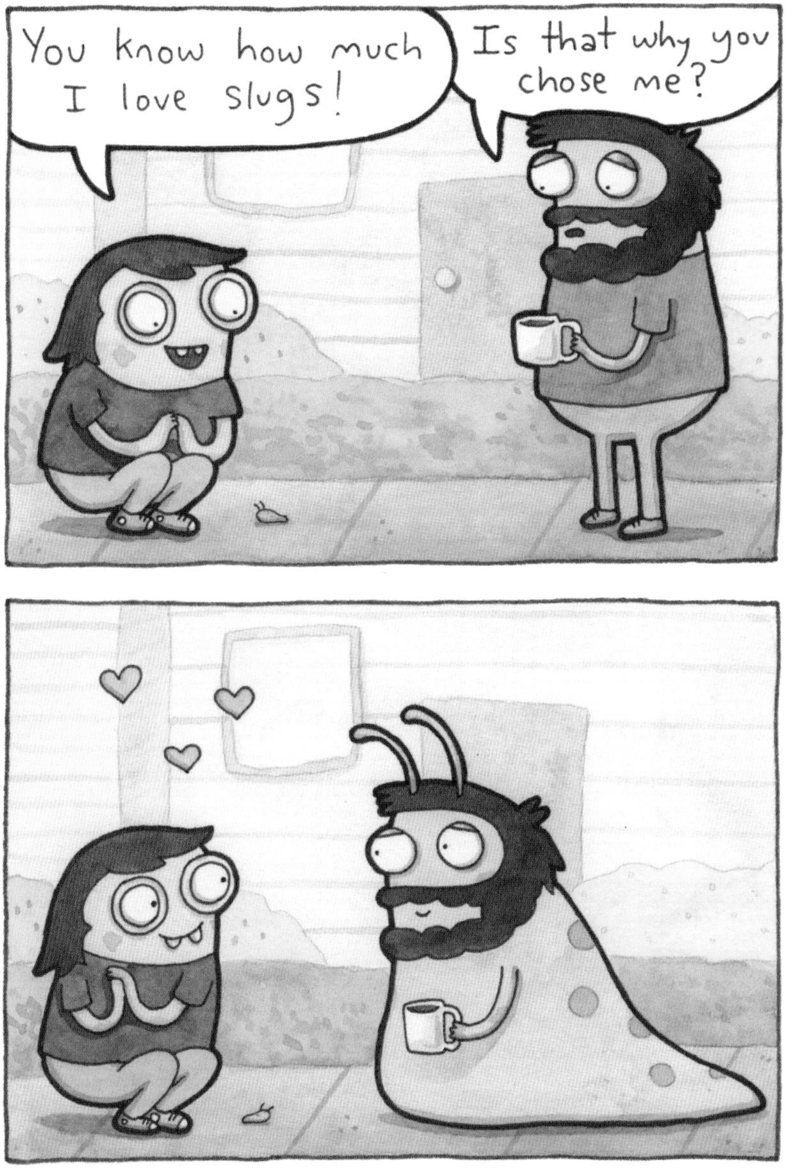
You know how much I love slugs!
Is that why you chose me?

I have a hard time asking for help.

Admitting I need help feels like admitting I'm broken.

Heh, this isn't so bad.

I don't want to be broken.

If I'm broken, what if I can't be fixed?

I'm starting to realize...

... asking for help doesn't mean I'm broken.
Umm guys?
It means I'm brave for knowing what I need.
And there's nothing broken about that.
Oh dear.

## A Few Of My Favorite Things

Being outside so long, it feels like I earned going inside.

Those little bumps on kids' new teeth.

Watching the intensity of the light change outside my window.

Crinkled car antennas.

Broken back windshield wipers.

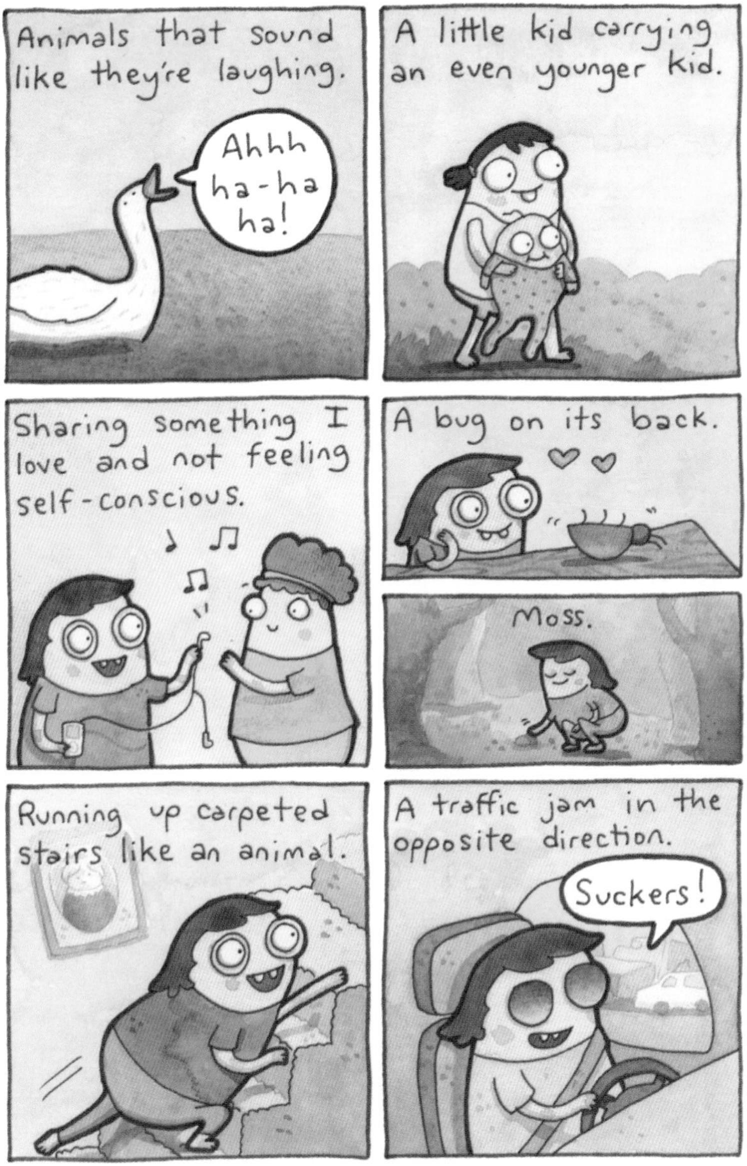
Animals that sound like they're laughing.
Ahhh ha-ha ha!
A little kid carrying an even younger kid.
Sharing something I love and not feeling self-conscious.
A bug on its back.
Moss.
Running up carpeted stairs like an animal.
A traffic jam in the opposite direction.
Suckers!

# Better Camera

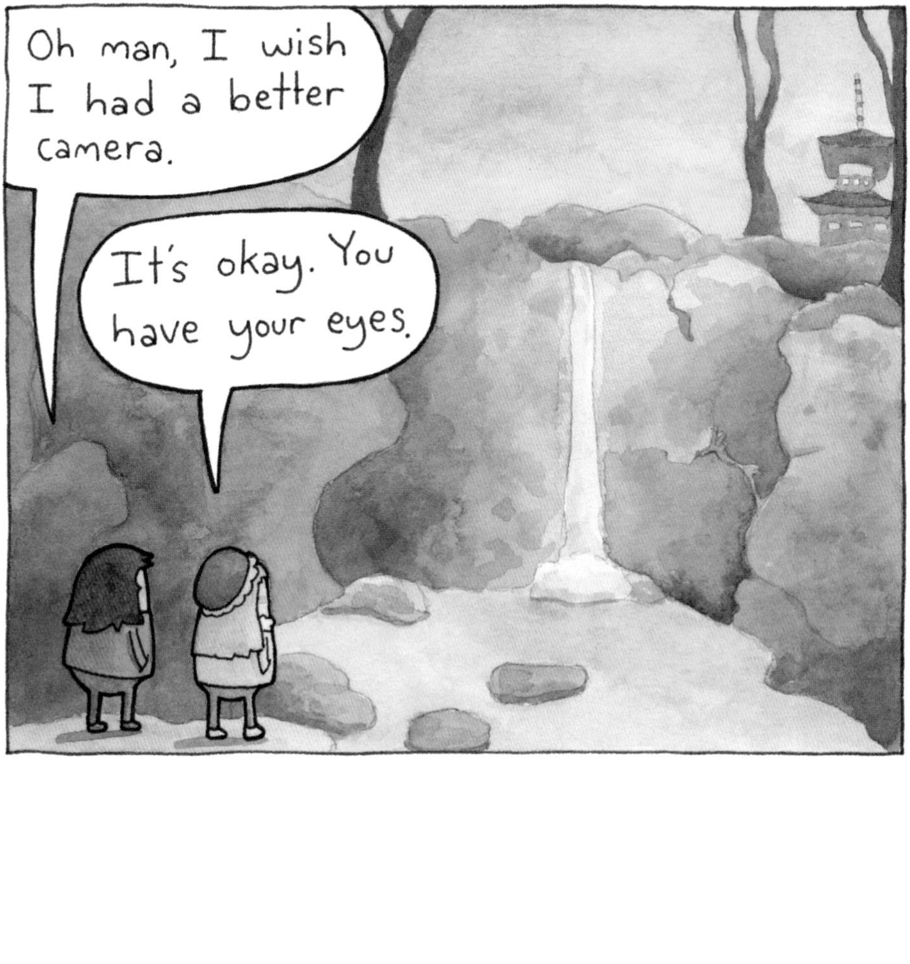
Oh man, I wish I had a better camera.
It's okay. You have your eyes.

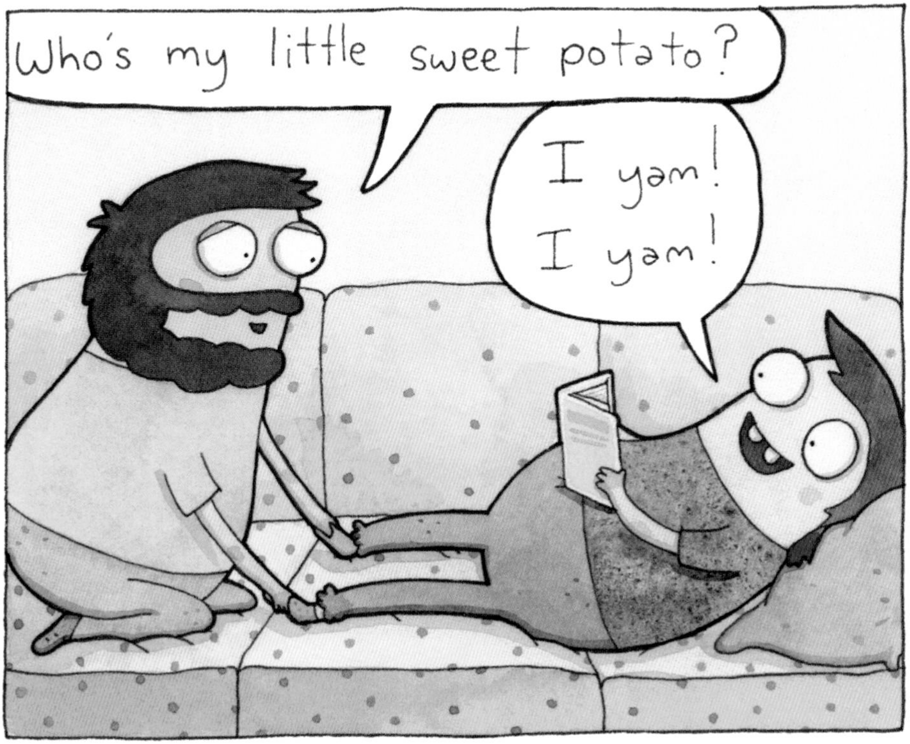
Who's my little sweet potato?
I yam! I yam!

# The Oboe

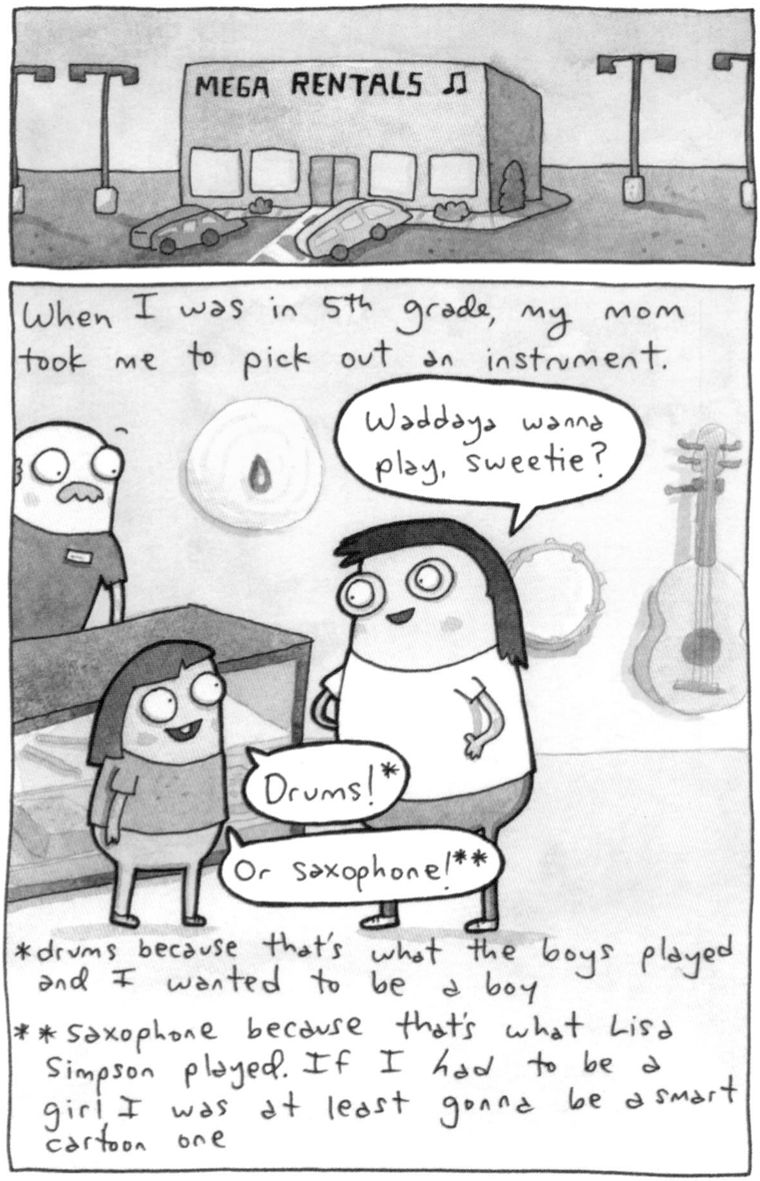
MEGA RENTALS ♫
When I was in 5th grade, my mom took me to pick out an instrument.
Waddaya wanna play, sweetie?
Drums!*
Or saxophone!**
*drums because that's what the boys played and I wanted to be a boy
**saxophone because that's what Lisa Simpson played. If I had to be a girl I was at least gonna be a smart cartoon one

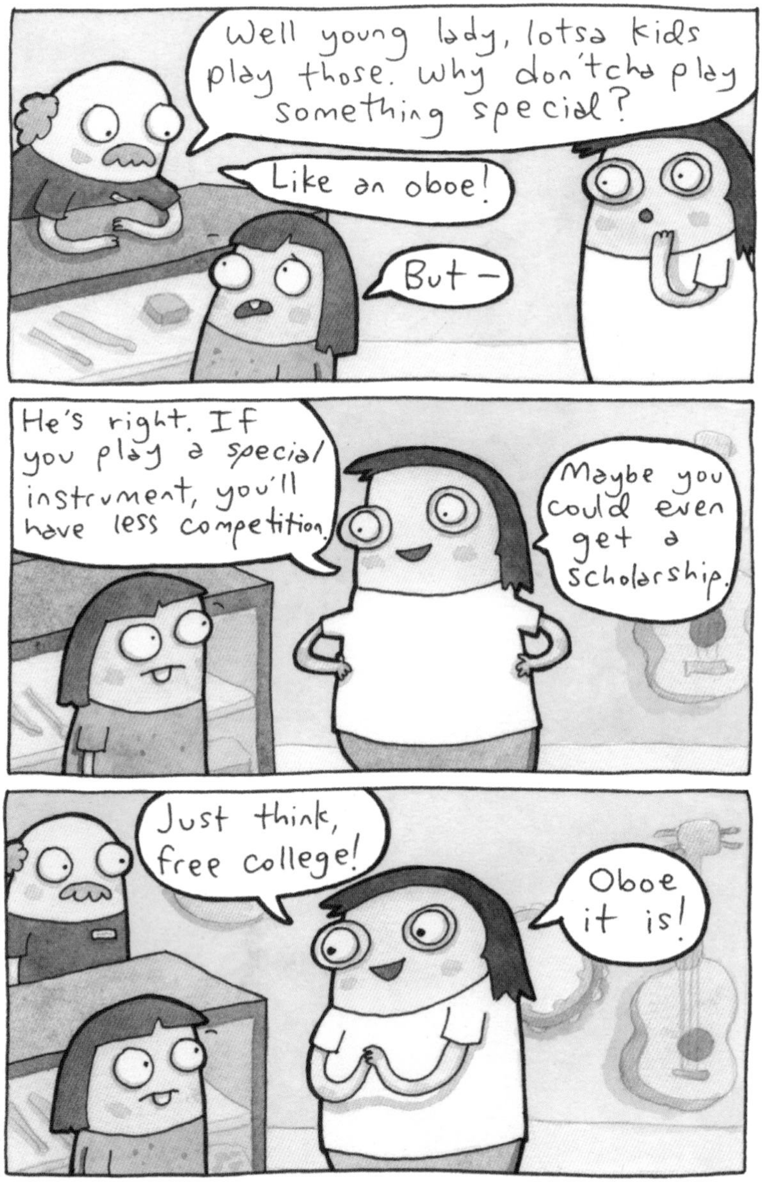
Well young lady, lotsa kids play those. Why don'tcha play something special?
Like an oboe!
But –
He's right. If you play a special instrument, you'll have less competition.
Maybe you could even get a scholarship.
Just think, free college!
Oboe it is!

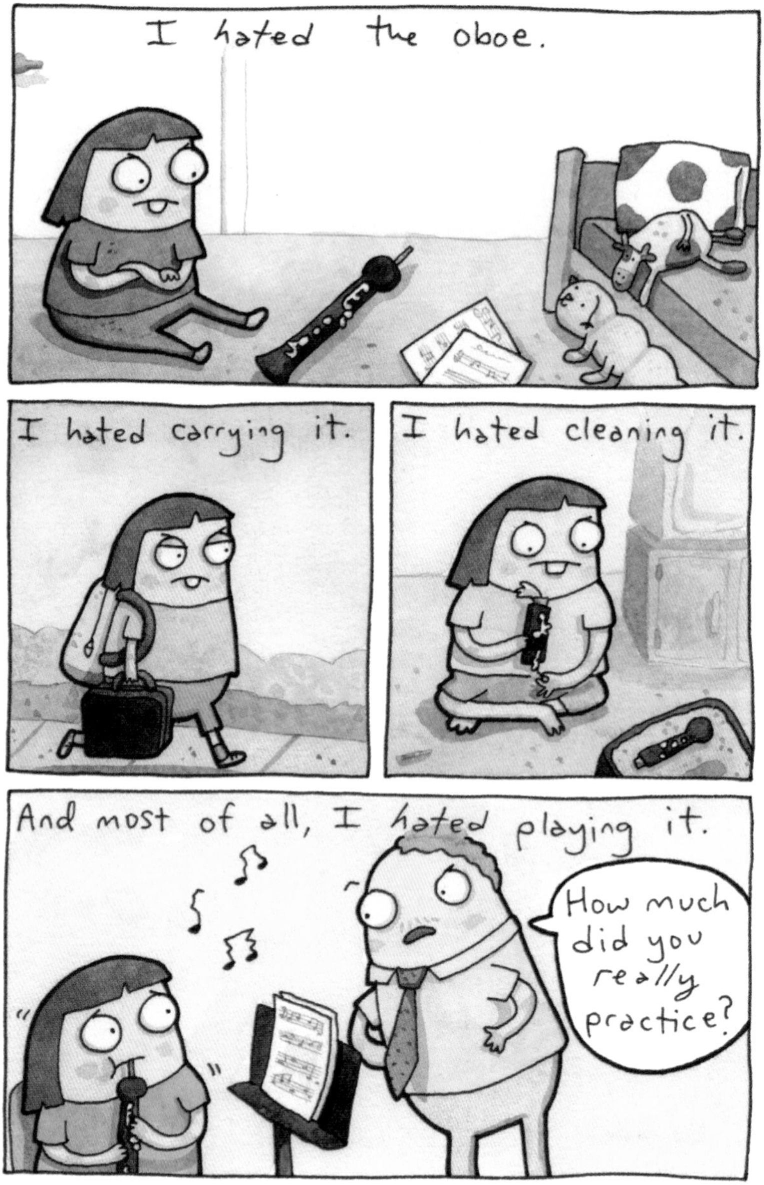
I hated the oboe.
I hated carrying it.
I hated cleaning it.
And most of all, I hated playing it.
How much did you really practice?

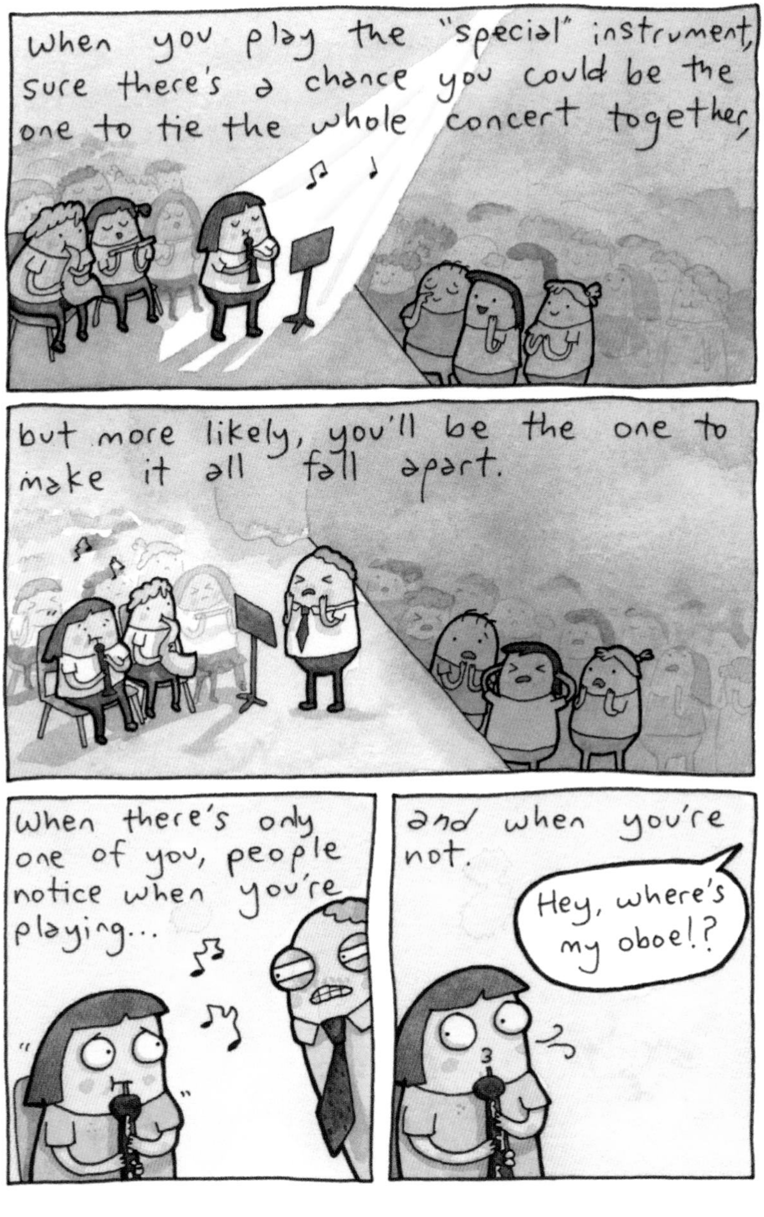
when you play the "special" instrument, sure there's a chance you could be the one to tie the whole concert together,
but more likely, you'll be the one to make it all fall apart.
when there's only one of you, people notice when you're playing...
and when you're not.
Hey, where's my oboe!?

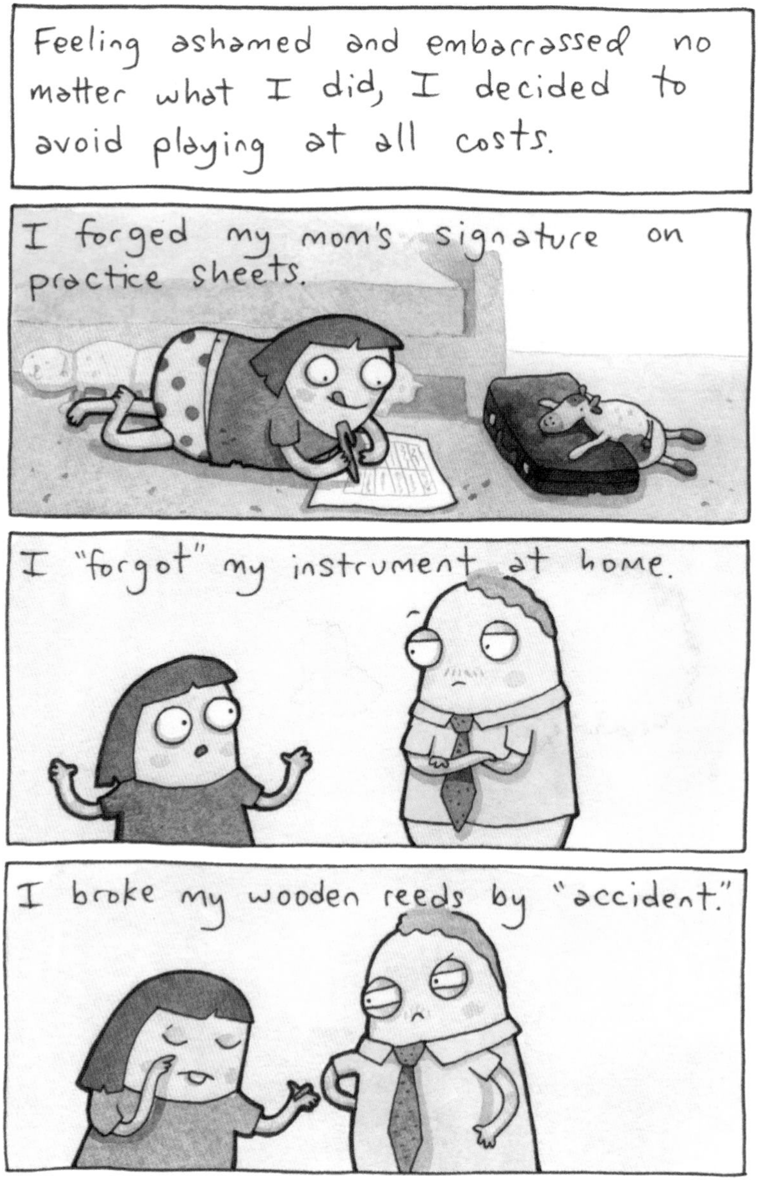
Feeling ashamed and embarrassed no matter what I did, I decided to avoid playing at all costs.
I forged my mom's signature on practice sheets.
I "forgot" my instrument at home.
I broke my wooden reeds by "accident."

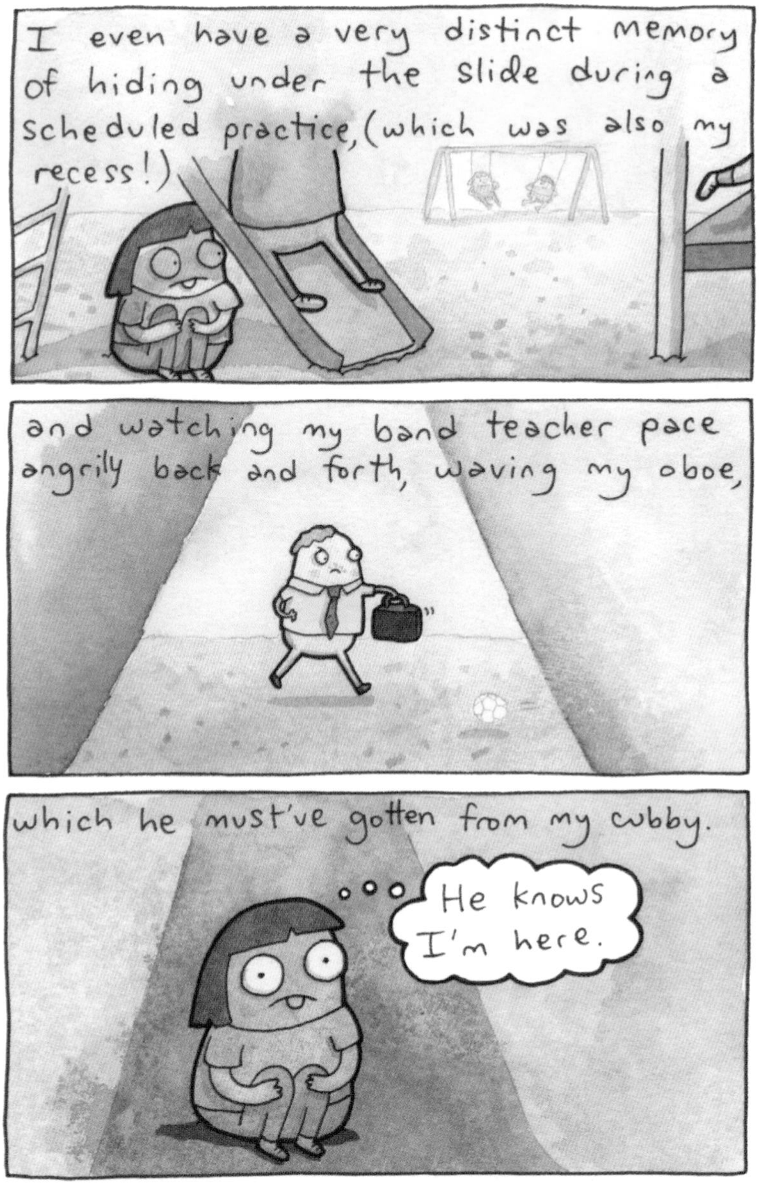
I even have a very distinct memory of hiding under the slide during a scheduled practice, (which was also my recess!)
and watching my band teacher pace angrily back and forth, waving my oboe,
which he must've gotten from my cubby.
He knows I'm here.

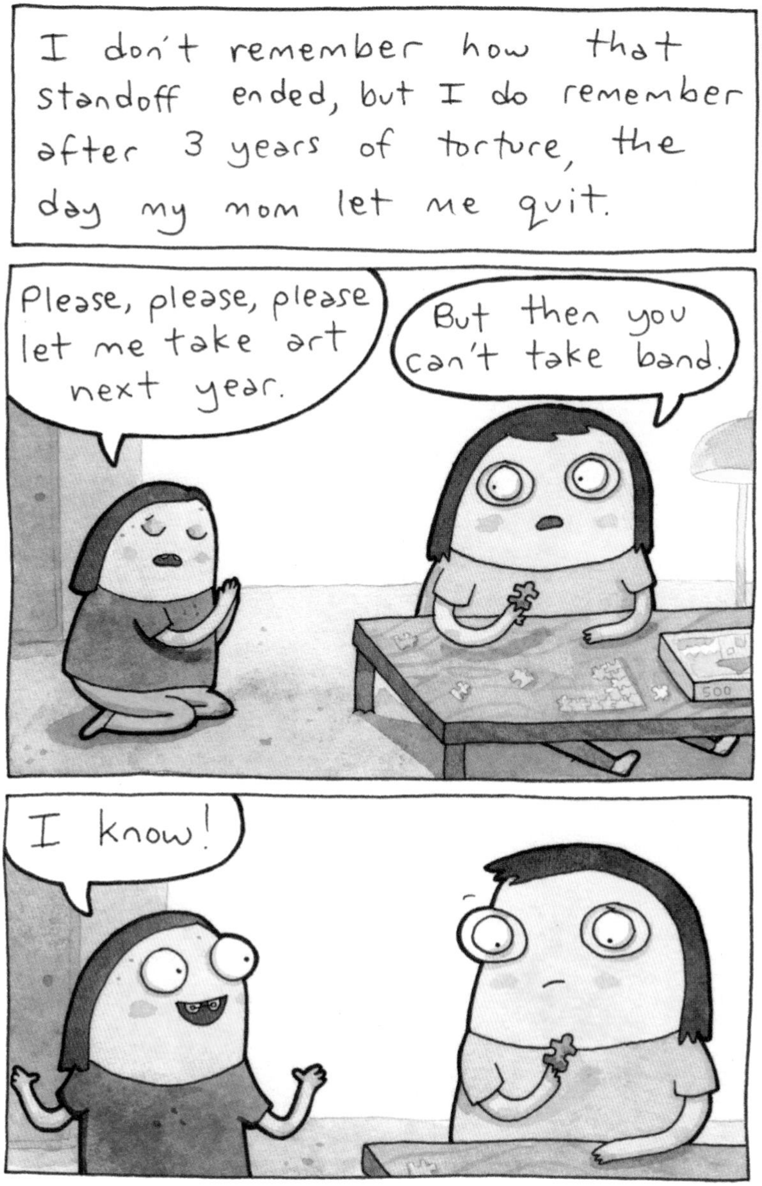
I don't remember how that standoff ended, but I do remember after 3 years of torture, the day my mom let me quit.
Please, please, please let me take art next year.
But then you can't take band.
500
I know!

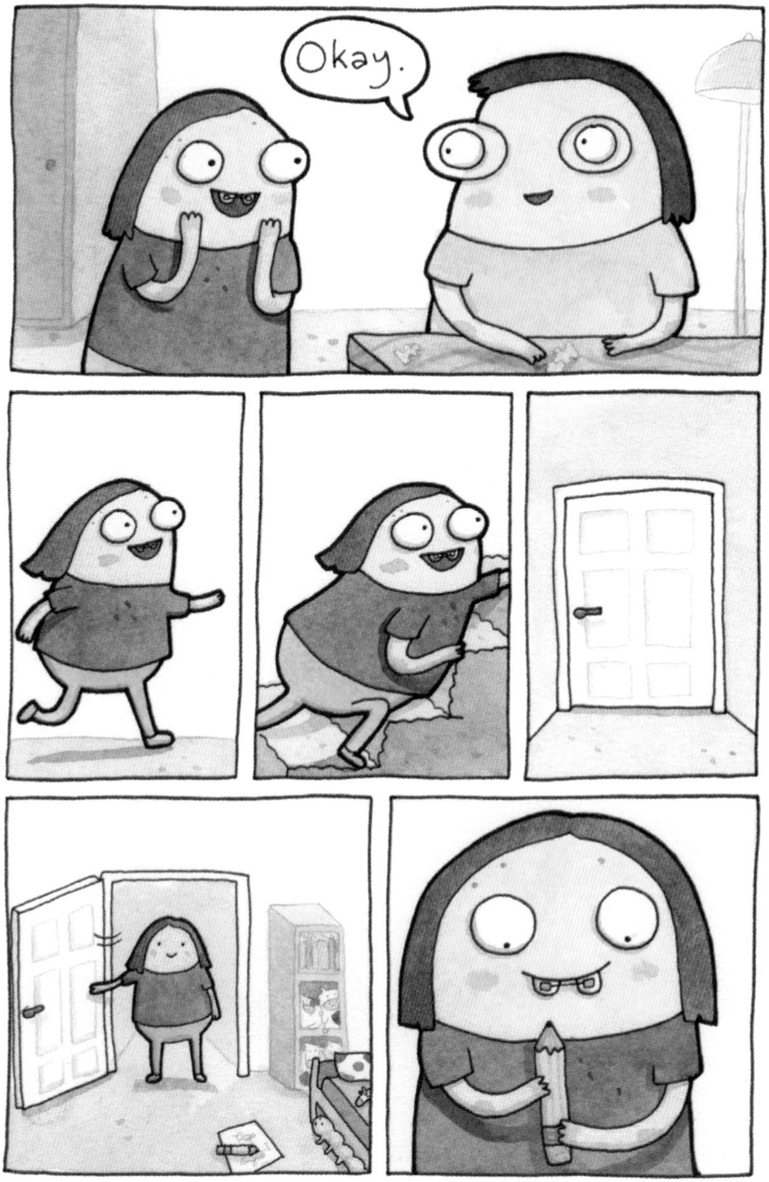
Okay.

# Believe in Magic

People don't understand me.
You're a unicorn.
Whether they can see it or not.
Don't waste your time trying to convince people who you are...
When they don't believe in magic.

# Fireflies

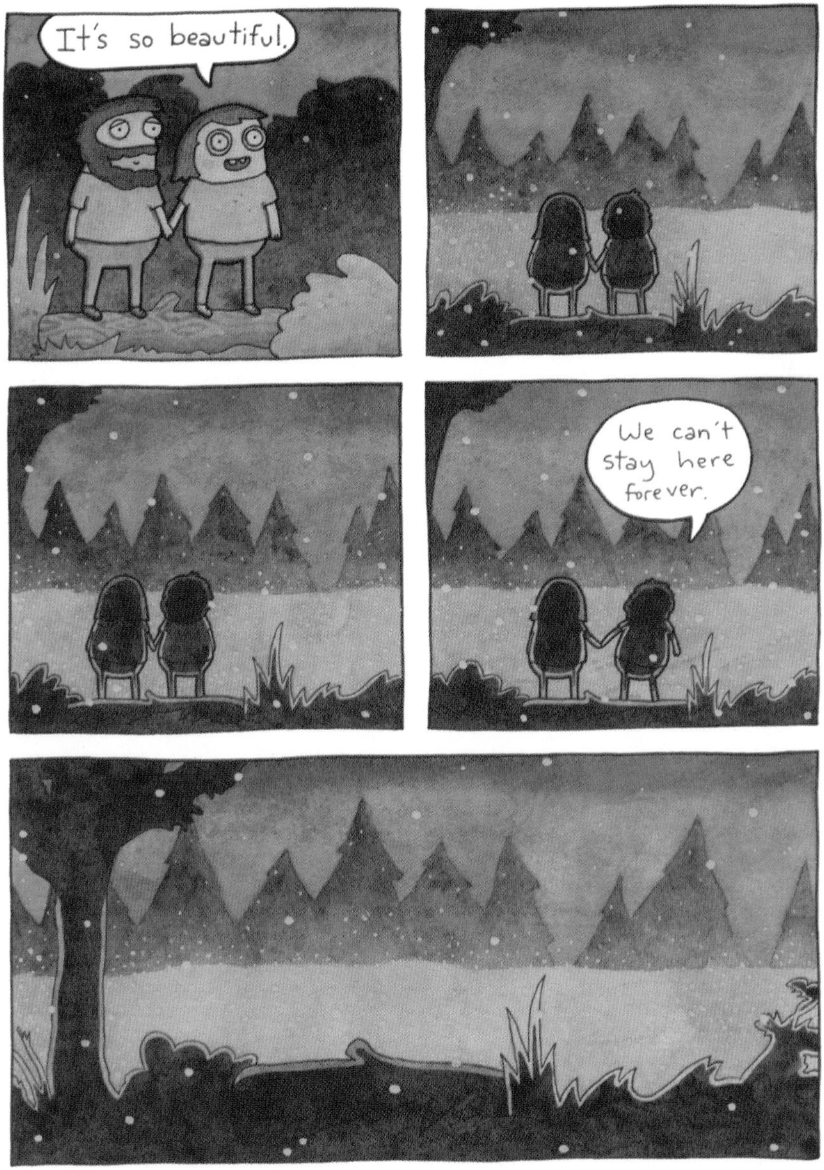
It's so beautiful.
We can't stay here forever.

# Better Half

Whenever I make a sandwich, I cut it super unevenly.
ssslice
I always leave the bigger half
munch munch
Hissss
so I can eat it last.

Making a diary comic can be exhausting.

It's like looking for gems inside of myself

then inspecting them to see if they're good enough.

Hmm this might work....

The deeper I dig, the more I find.

Phew

But it isn't always gems.

self-doubt

Sometimes I find really scary things.

unhealthy coping mechanisms

the compulsion to make fun of myself

difficulty setting boundaries

wanting to control everything

I'm realizing it's too much to deal with on my own,

holding myself to impossible standards

taking things too personally

discomfort with a range of emotions

So I'm inviting some friends to help

...and maybe a therapist.

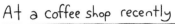

At a coffee shop recently

Here ya go.

Thanks!

Also... I read your comics and I've been meaning to tell you...

They make me feel less alone.

It's things like that that make me feel less alone

including each and every one of you.

Okay, you can go now.

# Travel Goals

I'm gonna get so much done traveling this weekend.
B5

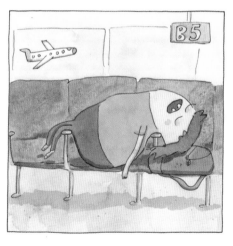

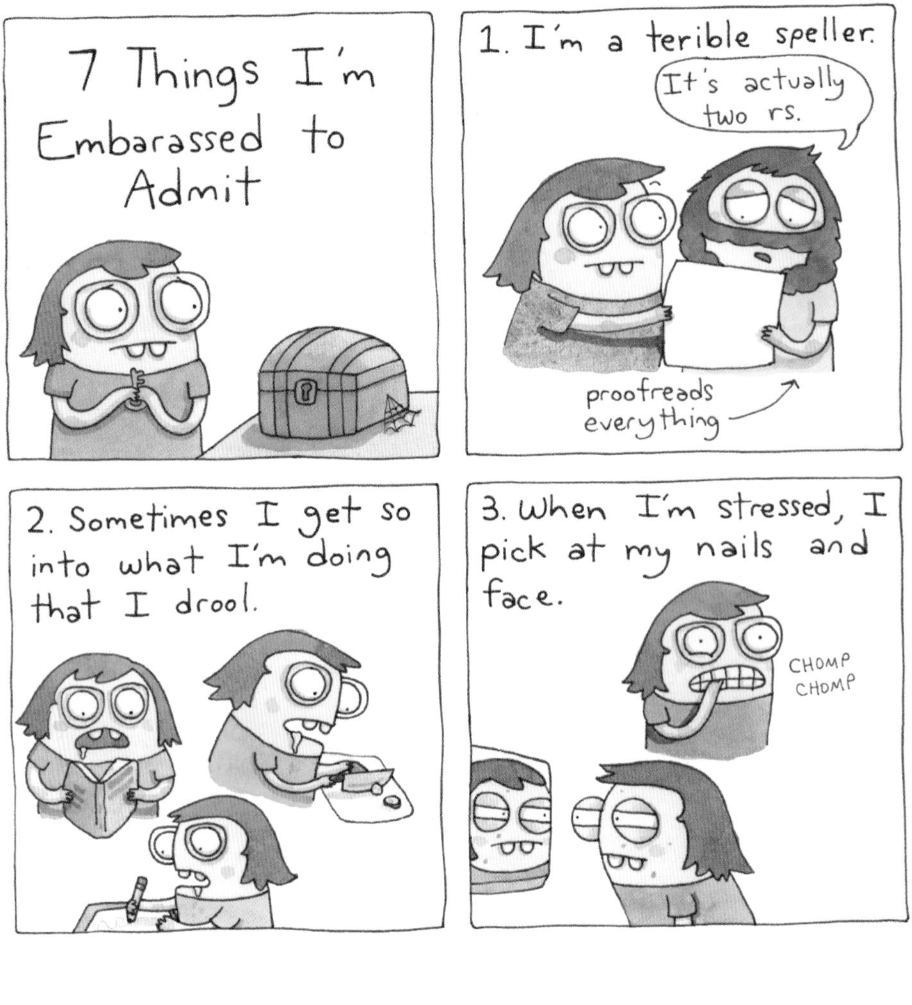
7 Things I'm Embarassed to Admit
1. I'm a teribble speller.
It's actually two rs.
proofreads everything
2. Sometimes I get so into what I'm doing that I drool.
3. When I'm stressed, I pick at my nails and face.
CHOMP CHOMP

4. Sometimes I do something nice just so I'll get something nice in return.

Say, ya need a ride to the airport?

Actually yeah that'd be great.

needs a ride in one week

5. I'm attracted to people in turtlenecks.

6. I have to poop the second I take a bite of breakfast.

How is it?

7. I'm making this whole comic artist thing up as I go.

Weeeee!

## The Cosmos

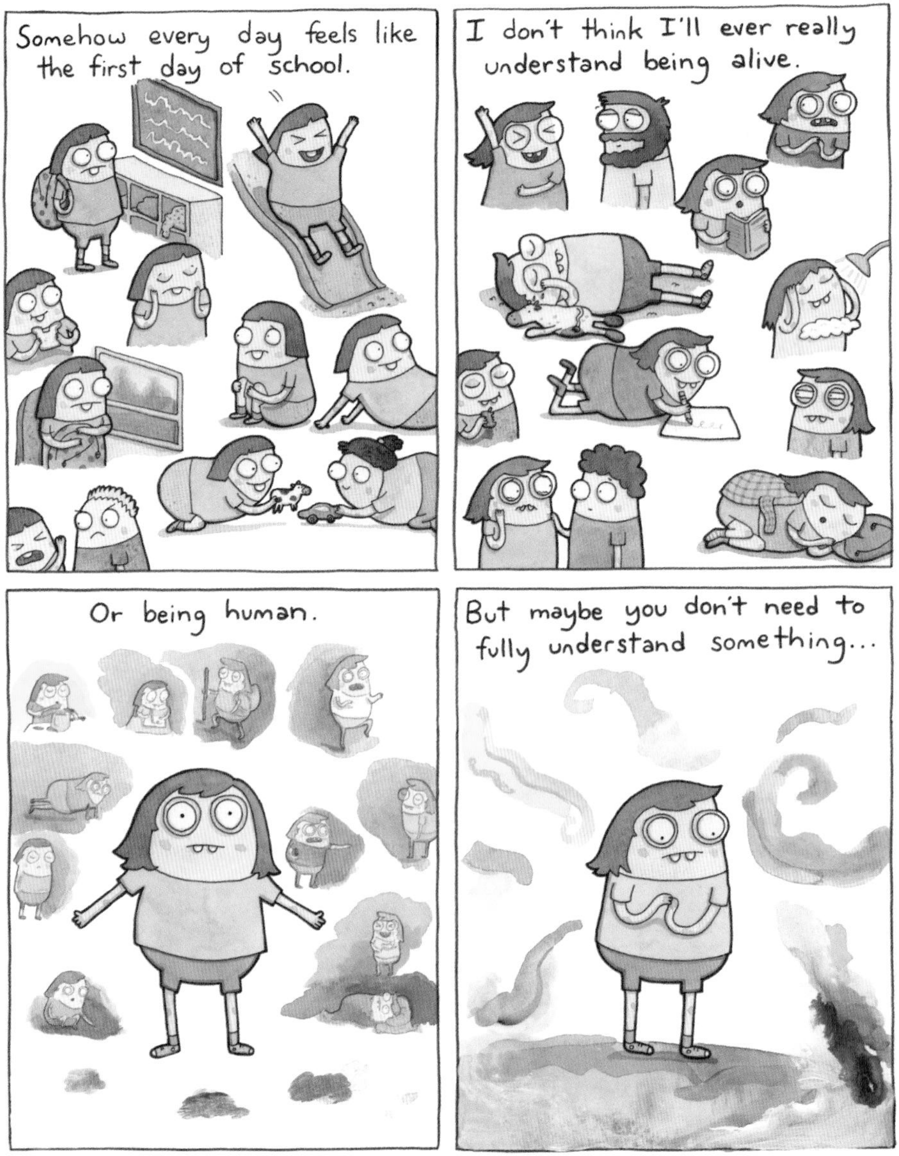
Somehow every day feels like the first day of school.
I don't think I'll ever really understand being alive.
Or being human.
But maybe you don't need to fully understand something...

to be part of it.

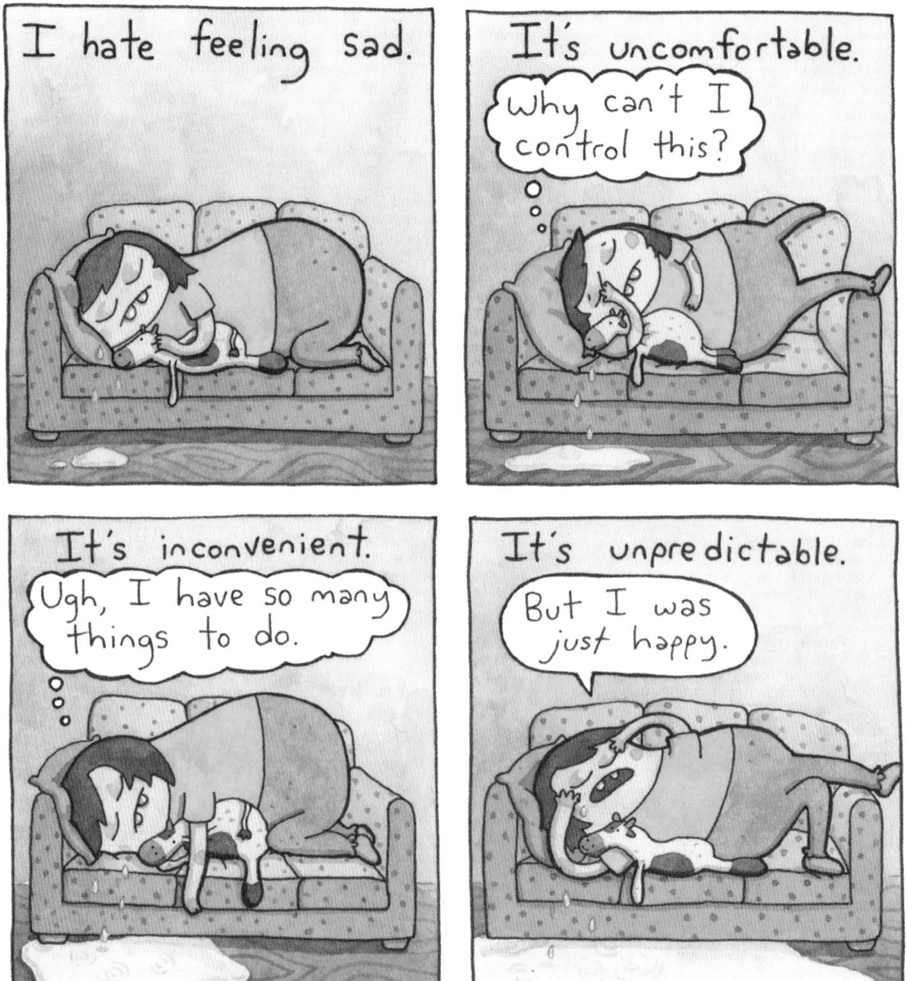
I hate feeling sad.
It's uncomfortable.
Why can't I control this?
It's inconvenient.
Ugh, I have so many things to do.
It's unpredictable.
But I was just happy.

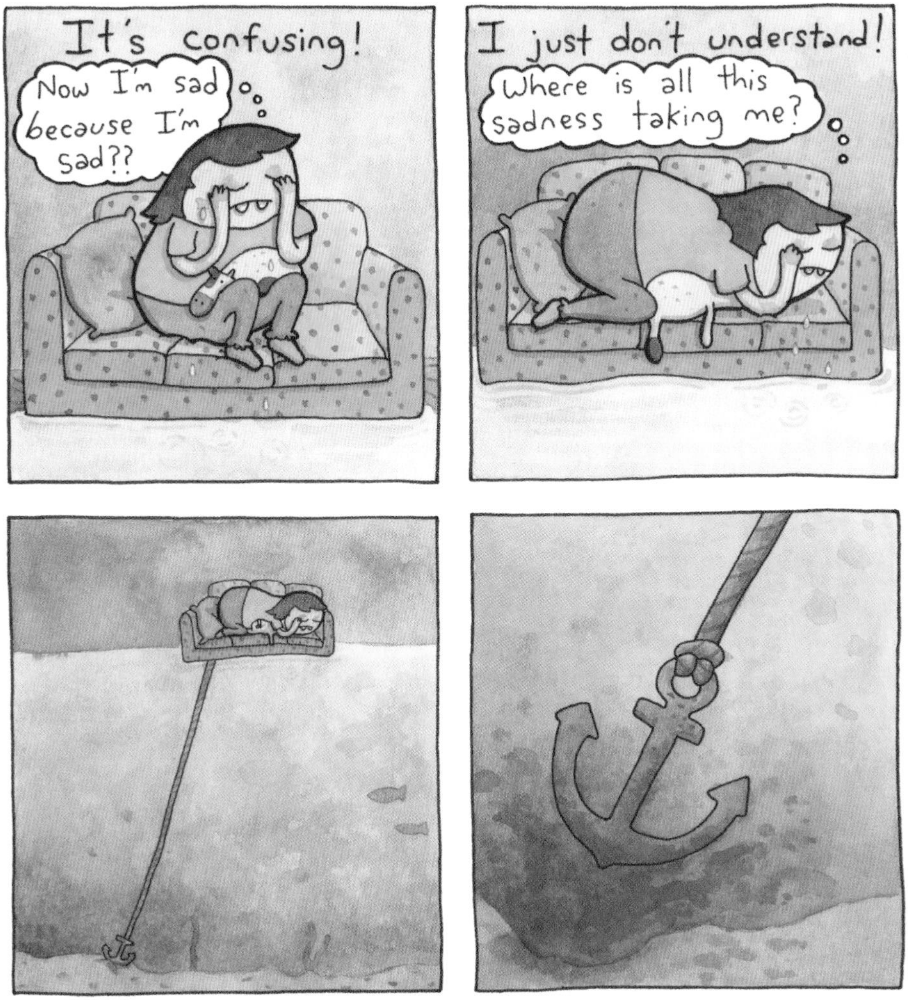
It's confusing!
Now I'm sad because I'm sad??
I just don't understand!
Where is all this sadness taking me?

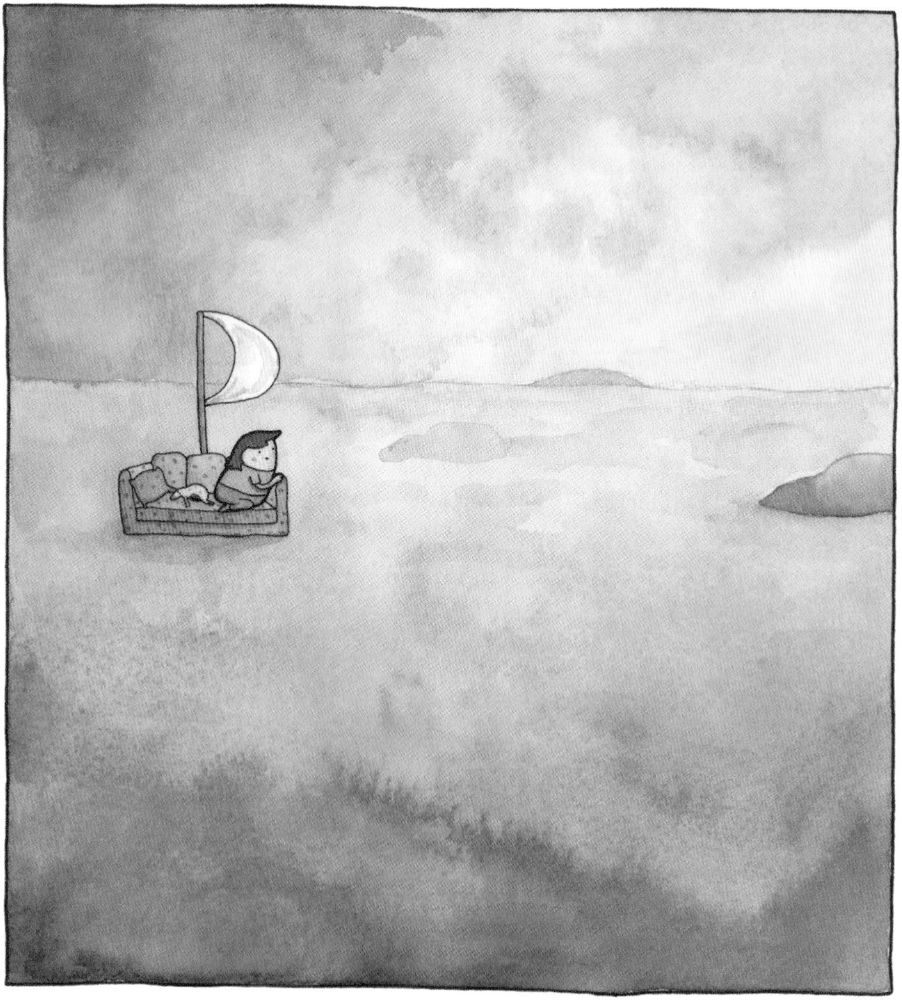

# I Get to Decide

Is this loneliness...
or alone time?
I get to decide

## The Way

Psst, follow me.
Just because someone shows me the way...
doesn't mean they *know* the way.

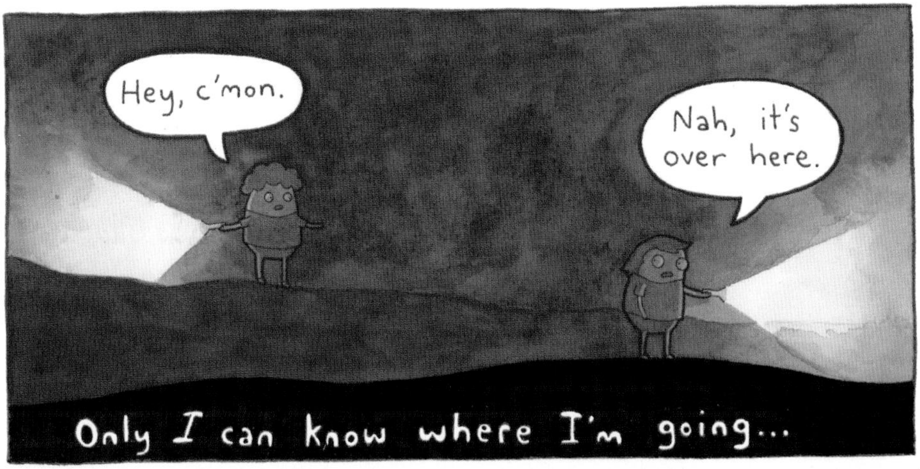
Hey, c'mon.
Nah, it's over here.
Only I can know where I'm going...

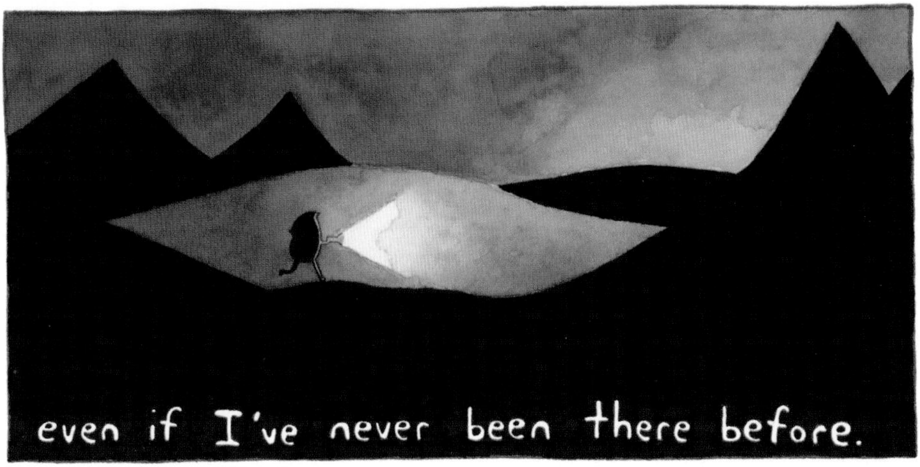
even if I've never been there before.

# About the Author

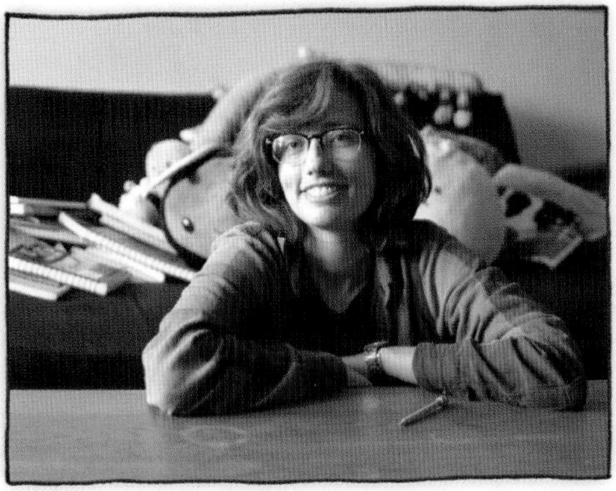

Jackie lives and works in a cozy one-bedroom apartment (heat's included!) in Rochester, New York, with an assortment of houseplant pals, plush toy companions, and one human husband, Pat. He's the tired purple character and a kindred, artistic spirit. Jackie enjoys personifying objects, meeting new people, breathing in the smell of the woods, and making large quantities of food to eat all week so she has more time to play in her sketchbook.

Butter Udder lives on Jackie's side of the bed and continues to work as an emotional support bovine. She greatly enjoys the benefits of being a tenured plush toy, including an annual bathing, a tiny vest at Christmas time that Jackie forced her mom to sew one year, and infinite snuggles. Although their relationship was tense at first, Butter Udder and Pat have managed to develop a mutual respect for each other. Some would even say, a fondness.

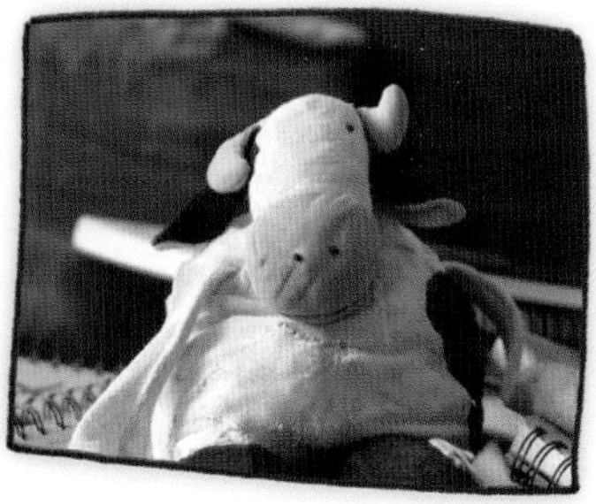

Follow Jackie 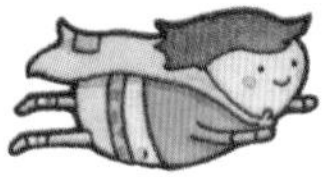

@underpantsandoverbites

@underpantsandoverbites

@underpantsandoverbites

underpantsandoverbites.com

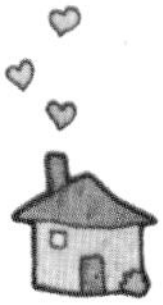